Warrior Princess: A People's Biography of Ida B. Wells

Warrior Princess

A People's Biography of Ida B. Wells

TODD STEVEN BURROUGHS

DIASPORIC AFRICA PRESS
NEW YORK

This book is a publication of
Diasporic Africa Press
New York | www.dafricapress.com

Copyright @ Diasporic Africa Press 2017

All rights reserved. No part of this publication may be reproduced or distributed in any form or by any means, or stored in a database or retrieval system, without the prior written permission of the publisher. The original version of this book was published on imixwhatilike.org.

Library of Congress Control Number: 2017954248
ISBN-13 978-1-937306-60-1 (pbk.: alk paper)

To my sensei, Dr. Vicky Gholson (1950-2014), a creative genius and largely unsung hero who was In the Tradition of the 20th and 21st century Harlem activist, intellectual, artist, and visionary

CONTENTS

INTRODUCTION 1

CHAPTER ONE: *A Post-Civil War Life of Hope, Destroyed by Plague; Parents and an Adolescence Stolen* 9

CHAPTER TWO: *Miss Ida B. Wells, The Schoolteacher Who Fought on a Train* 15

CHAPTER THREE: *The Shaping of Black America: Ida B. Wells, the Black Press and Free Speech in Post-reconstruction Memphis* 23

CHAPTER FOUR: *Knotted Rope: Wells' Campaigns Against Lynching* 43

CHAPTER FIVE: *The 'Princess Of The Press' Becomes a Feted Clubwoman* 79

CHAPTER SIX: *Ida's Alphabet: NAACP, NACW, NFL, NERL* 89

CHAPTER SEVEN: *Family Time* 103

CHAPTER EIGHT: *Sexism in the Movement: Wells-Barnett Fights Black Female Invisibilty* 111

CHAPTER NINE: *The Complicated*

Relationship Between Wells-Barnett and White Feminism 121

CHAPTER TEN: *An Elder in the 20th Century Black Freedom Movement* 137

CODA: *A Nation of Leading Black Female Voices* 147

BIBLIOGRAPHY 181

INTRODUCTION

Ida B. Wells-Barnett (1862-1931) has gone from mid-twentieth century obscurity to a major twenty-first century subject in Women's Studies and the history of Black American media.

Her life was much more complex than the one paragraph portrait written of her: Black journalist, anti-lynching crusader. She was first and foremost a mother and wife. She was also a local Chicago community activist for decades.

She was a devout Christian who believed deeply in the Black church and in Black schools, even when those institutions didn't believe in her. She had no problem publicly criticizing Black ministers who failed to represent their flocks, and Black school systems when they failed the students in her charge. She would be fired and ostracized by many elements of the Black community for her stands.

She was a major leader of several movements: the suffragist movement, the Black women's club movement, as well as the National Association for the Advancement of Colored People. She was maneuvered out of power in many of the movements she led. It was especially despicable that, as the NAACP became more and more involved in anti-lynching, she was left out of its history, erased from the cause for which she risked her life!

Her independent spirit infused her work. She went out and did her own investigative reports on lynching. She wrote articles for Black newspapers, a relatively new vehicle that came out of Northern antebellum Black nationalism and the abolitionist movement, and she wrote pamphlets—small booklets that allowed her to narrate in detail what she saw, documented and believed about lynching.

Because of this independence, she was held at a distance by both Black male leaders and white female leaders—and sometimes even by Black women leaders. Was it because she was a no-nonsense person who didn't suffer fools easily? Partly, but it was also because she could be intimidating, and many leaders wanted the spotlight for themselves. It was also because she lived and fought during the dominance of two Black leadership pillars: first, Booker T. Washington, and second, the white liberals and Black men who controlled the National NAACP.

Wells-Barnett never gave up writing and organizing. She relished a good fight her entire life. With the broken promises of Reconstruction, she had plenty of opportunities.

She is the historic link between Harriet Tubman, the great abolitionist and Civil War hero, and Ethel Payne, the pioneering twentieth century Chicago Black journalist who took up the journalism role she had pioneered. She lived during the time of the birth of Jim Crow and died 24 years before Rosa Parks refused to give up her bus seat to a white man, spurring the mass-action wing of the Civil Rights Movement. But by the time she died, white women and Black northern men and women had the right to vote, the NAACP was on its way to becoming the most powerful civil rights organization of all time, and the Black press, thanks to the societal changes of the twentieth century, was about to become the most powerful non-religious institution in Black communities.

Ida B. Wells-Barnett fought attempts to forget her while she lived. In addition to her articles, she wrote an autobiography, posthumously edited by her daughter. In the more than 80 years since her death, she has been the subject of at least three scholarly biographies, including a major one by a Black woman scholar, Paula Giddings. She was the subject of a PBS "American Experience" documentary: *Ida B. Wells: A Passion for Justice*, which aired in 1989. Her diary has been published, as well as a major collection of her journalism.

Wells was as fierce as Frederick Douglass, as important an activist as W.E.B. Du Bois, as innovative as Booker T. Washington and as powerful an advocacy journalist as William Monroe Trotter. But because she was a woman, she had been marginalized as a contemporary as well as a historic figure after her death.

She would be proud to know that her life and work has, in the twenty-first century, become a major landmark of nineteenth century anti-lynching studies, Black studies, Women's Studies, and Feminist Studies.

This work is not a work of biography as much as it an ideological portrait from a Black feminist perspective. It's a book that discusses the ideas and institutions around Ida B. Wells-Barnett as she spent her life in teaching, journalism, anti-lynching campaigns, and civil rights and political organizing. It discusses how she balanced white racism of both genders, and sexism from Black male leaders. It attempts to show how one Black woman created and maintained her selfhood amidst such challenges.

This book is for Black women activists of the twenty-first century—those who are committed to showing that Black lives have always mattered most to them. It is for the young Black women who have spearheaded major protests and demonstrations during the presidencies of both Barack Obama, a Black Democrat, and Donald Trump, a white Republican. I want the struggles within this book to resonate with them.

Wells-Barnett's personal history tells us not only that there's no easy road, but no reward for standing for the basics of civilization. It shows that victory does not equal celebration or credit. That when you use a sword to cut down injustice, the people who pass through the barriers you broke can have selective amnesia.

Black female activism is a curious thing. Black women don't posture, they build. Black women don't win; they rescue. Their reward is the stability of the Black family and the Black community. Other than equality, Ida B. Wells-Barnett wanted nothing more than that.

She was not afraid of the consequences of being open and active to get what she wanted. Her struggles were not only against enemies, but also against friends like the NAACP, who wanted her present but quiet; not only against white male racists who wanted to kill her, but also against white women who wanted her literally in the back of the suffragist march line.

Ida B. Wells-Barnett demanded her own terms in life. She got them; she lived the life she wanted. But it was always a struggle, and the only reward was being able to express herself and live her own values in a deeply repressive time.

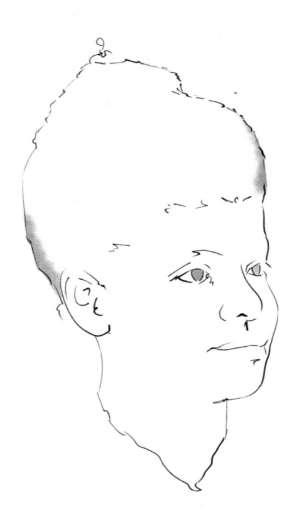

CHAPTER ONE
A Post-Civil War Life of Hope, Destroyed by Plague; Parents and an Adolescence Stolen

Ida Bell Wells, one of the freest Black women of the late nineteenth and early twentieth century, was born into slavery on July 16, 1862, to enslaved parents, in Holly Springs, Mississippi. She was the eldest of eight.

Her parents, James Wells and Elizabeth Warrenton Wells, were filled with hope for the free future that came with the Emancipation Proclamation of 1863 and the end of the Civil War in 1865. The couple had been married as enslaved persons, but they got married again as free people.

James had skills from slavery that transferred into his new freeman life. James was the son of his master, Morgan Wells. He became a carpenter because Morgan made him learn the trade for use on the plantation. James' mother was named Peggy, and she was a slave.

Elizabeth, who, as a young woman, had been sold along with her two sisters, was a homemaker, a well-reputed cook (she met her husband because she was the cook to the white man from whom James learned carpentry), and a devoted Sunday School attendee.[1]

Besides Ida, the other children were: Alfred James, George, Eugenia, Eddie, Annie, Lily, and Stanley.

The Wells family lived in a single-story, three-room house James built. After the Civil War, Hollis Springs became one of the Freedman Bureau's regional headquarters. The Freedman's Bureau was set up by President Lincoln after the war to assist the formerly enslaved Africans with all necessities, from food to medical supplies and labor contracts.

Other than the local Black church, Rust University (originally named Shaw University) played a central role in the Wells family life. Rust taught all grade levels, an important mandate for the newly freed

African people. James was a university trustee, and Elizabeth, wanting to learn how to read so she could read the Bible, attended school with her children. Because on Sundays only the Bible could be read, Ida read the book repeatedly.[2]

—§—

Ida was on her grandmother's farm when the yellow fever devastated the town of approximately 3,500 in September of 1878. The disease snatched James, Elizabeth and Ida's youngest sibling Stanley from the family.[3] The Wellses were now a family of six orphans, since Eddie had died of spinal meningitis previously.

The brotherhood of Masons—honoring their Brother James, who had become a Master Mason—stepped forward. At a meeting, they agreed that Ida was old enough to be on her own, so the remaining children were going to be divided up among them.

Ida was 16 at the time, and found out about the arrangement. She told the gathering that the family was going to stay together, under her leadership. "I said that it would make my father and mother turn over in their graves to know their children had been scattered like that and that we owned the house and if the Masons would help me find work, I would take care of them."[4]

She ended her adolescence sharply. She dropped out of Rust, passed the teaching exam, changed her appearance (including lowering her dress hem line), and morphed into an 18-year-old adult teacher, a responsible breadwinner. "After being a happy, light-hearted schoolgirl," recalled Ida, "I suddenly found myself at the head of a family."[5]

She taught in a rural area near Holly Springs for a time, and the remaining children came to stay with Ida and their grandmother a short time later. Sadly, the grandmother had a stroke and Eugenia, who was physically disabled, died within two years.

Ida's aunt, Fanny Butler, invited her and her two younger sisters to come live in Memphis. She offered to take care of Annie and Lily. (George and Alfred James were sent to live with relatives; they ultimately became carpenters.) The hellish transition period—the grief of losing first their parents, and now Eugenia gone and their grandmother being stricken and unable to help—had come to an end. Ida would establish an evolving identity in Memphis: first as a schoolteacher, then as a defendant in a well-publicized civil rights trial and at first concurrently, and finally, as a writer.

With the tragedy that already had visited her, and the very adult decision she had to make because of that most personal calamity, Ida B. Wells already was quite familiar with the pain and responsibilities of life. (As her biographer, Paula Giddings, described: "Wells had left Holly Springs deeply marked by the grief and anger rooted in her abandonment [.]"[6]) She was about to learn firsthand of its dangers and promise in ways that would define the young woman, publicly and privately, for the entire span of her lifetime.

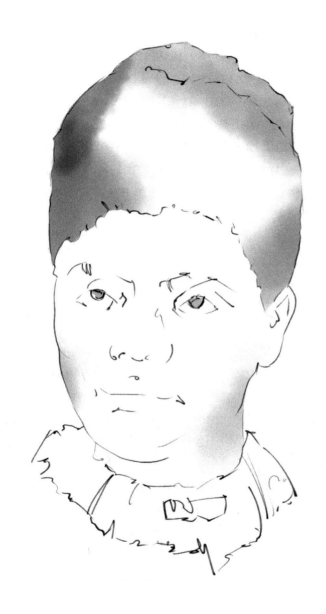

CHAPTER TWO
Miss Ida B. Wells, the Schoolteacher Who Fought on a Train

Wells had become an adult and a teacher in just two years. She initially taught at a school in Woodstock, a town near Memphis. Her sisters were cared for by Aunt Fanny in Memphis, so she commuted and could stay in Woodstock. Then she taught in Shelby County, Tennessee, because the pay was a little bit better. By 1884, though, she had passed her Memphis exams and was a fulltime part of the city's (Colored) school system.

It was an exciting time for the young woman because in the city, she could develop her intellectual interests (she had always been an avid reader; she claimed to have read all the books in the Hollis Springs Sunday school library and the ones at Rust University), enjoy entertainment such as concerts and plays (she was a lover of Shakespeare), and, eventually, write letters and editorials for religious weeklies. It was her first time living in a city with a large Black population.

She was approached by potential suitors. Wells was attractive and flirty, but also a devout Christian and very no-nonsense. Her diary shows a woman in search of a man she could respect and love. She worked on improving herself, loving herself, and trying to leave the resentment she felt about what had happened in Holly Springs behind her.

In Memphis, she was able to create a real life. It was, for an educated Black woman in the nineteenth century Jim Crow South, a full one.

Ida B. Wells became a schoolteacher during a time in which the promise of Reconstruction had been dashed. The new-found power of Black elected officials was taken back because of the Tilden-Hayes Compromise of 1877. The Northern troops left, and the white South was free to create its own racist society, one where Blacks would be disenfranchised and made afraid to compete with whites in any way. The newly-placed restrictions of Black life were backed up by white terrorist violence, most notably in the form of the Ku Klux Klan. But the violence that Wells would soon fight would be, de facto and de jure, sanctioned by the city of Memphis and the state of Tennessee.

But first she had to fight a train company. On September 15, 1883, Wells boarded the Covington train on the Chesapeake & Ohio Railway line. Because she had a first-class ticket, she moved from the "Colored" car to the ladies' car. She got into a dispute with a conductor when he demanded that she move to the Colored car. Wells refused because white people were drinking and smoking in the Colored car. After repeated demands, the conductor tried to physically move Wells from her seat. She fastened her feet to the seat in front of her, and bit the conductor's hand. The conductor got help from the white passengers to dislodge Wells. She chose to get off the train rather than go into the dirty, smoky, Colored car. The white passengers cheered. Wells took the case to Circuit Court, where she won the case in 1884, but the Tennessee Supreme Court in 1887 reversed the decision.[7] She vented in her diary: "I felt so disappointed, because I had hoped such great things from my suit for my people generally. I have firmly believed all along that the law was on our side and would, when we appealed to it, give us justice. I feel shorn of that belief and utterly discouraged, and just now if it were possible would gather my race in my arms and fly away with them."[8]

Wells had become well-known because of the case. She had put her version about what happened to her in print. She did not see that action as having anything to do with her future; it was just a protest action.

Wells had come to push herself outward, into Memphis' Black community. She wanted friends and intellectual stimulation. So around 1885 she joined a literary society, called a lyceum. The one she joined, the Memphis Lyceum, had as members her school colleagues. The Vance Street Christian Church sessions on Friday afternoons, she wrote, "was a breath of life to me."[9] The meetings would always close with the editor of a local newspaper, *The Evening Star*, reciting a round-robin collection of interesting items. When the editor left for a job in Washington, D.C., it was Wells who was elected editor. "I tried to make my offering as acceptable as his," she wrote, "and before long I found that I liked the work."[10] One of the men who came to the lyceum was Rev. R.N. Countee, who had a church and edited a Christian weekly called *The Living Way*. Wells began to write for that paper as well. For *The Living Way*, she started writing a column expressing her opinions on the Black community's problems and what she saw as solutions. She created a pen name for these columns—"Iola."[11]

She had considered leaving Memphis—she points out that in 1886, she had taught "for one month in the states of California, Missouri and Tennessee"—but whether she disagreed with the new surroundings or the new surroundings disagreed with her, she kept coming back.[12] She belonged in Memphis. So did "Iola." While the schoolteacher Wells seemed stymied in her work, "Iola" was getting offers to write for more Black (and Black Christian) newspapers, going to (Colored) press association meetings, and being introduced to esteemed race leaders such as the journalist T. Thomas Fortune, and prophetic voices such as Bishop Henry McNeal Turner and Frederick Douglass. Eventually, "Iola" was nicknamed "The Princess of the Press." Back in Memphis, "Iola" was asked to be a writer for *The Free Speech and Headlight*. She only agreed if she could be one-third owner and editor. The year was 1889. The newspaper eventually would just be known as *The Free Speech*.[13]

Wells and "Iola" would soon be forced to merge. What happened first was that Wells lost her teaching job because of what "Iola" had written about the bad conditions of the Memphis school system.[14] So Wells became "Iola" fulltime.

But their real combined work was just around the bend, waiting somewhere in a field, hanging from a tree, far away from a ransacked Black grocery store. In 1892, there would be no turning back or turning away.

CHAPTER THREE
The Shaping of Black America: Ida B. Wells, The Black Press and Free Speech in Post-Reconstruction Memphis

Ida B. Wells was born, raised and came to adulthood through a period that historian Lerone Bennett Jr. calls the "founding" of Black America. The idea that Black Americans were—and are—a nation within a nation is not a new concept. Wells was a pragmatist, but as she became more active in Black journalism and boldly stepped into the dangerous public arena of white mob lynching, she began to see that Black unity was not just the best solution, but the only one.

Black America's Founding

Historian Lerone Bennett Jr. described the period between 1787 and 1837 as its most important thus far. During those years, with most African-Americans still enslaved, Black Americans struggled to build their own institutions to escape the virulent racism they lived with each day. The North's free Blacks and escaped slaves had developed several institutions. Churches, schools and clubs were the most common. The need to know each other and gather meant more than social advancement; it meant survival. Blacks were not allowed to mix with whites in any of those institutions, so Blacks had to build their own. Separated from Africa and by America, they began to think of themselves, as Bennett says, "as a common people with common aspirations and a common enemy."[15]

Bennett argued that Black America was founded by 1787 to 1837 by these free Blacks. Bennett divides the era of the founding of Black America into two time periods. The first, 1787 to 1816, was when free Northern Blacks began to found schools, lodges, churches and other institutions after the Revolutionary War.[16] The second period, 1817 to 1837, was when

Blacks had completed building their main institutions and began their agitation for full civil and human rights.[17]

The Beginning of Black Press History

One institution that developed during this second period was the Black press. Black newspapers were created to give these "founders" of Black America voices to publicly air their grievances. The Black press was founded to add a Black-controlled voice to the abolitionist movement. It also showed Black achievements and aspirations to the world. In so doing, it connected the various institutions and founders.

The Black press began in New York City in 1827, during that second period of Black America's founding. Two freedmen, Rev. Samuel Cornish and John Brown Russwurm, created the newspaper *Freedom's Journal*.

Other free Blacks began to publish newspapers or pamphlets.

Most notably in the period before Wells' *Free Speech* days were two publications in the United States:

- *David Walker's Appeal* (1829), a pamphlet that prophesized that God was going to punish white slaveholders, and
- *The North Star* (1847), the newspaper founded and edited by the former slave and great abolitionist Frederick Douglass.

But probably the most significant Black newspaper of North America, from the perspective of Black female journalism, happened in Canada. Mary Ann Shadd Cary, one of the emigrants to Canada because of the Fugitive Slave Act, edited *The Provincial Freeman*. The newspaper, which lasted from 1853 to 1858, promoted emigration and self-reliance. Her goal was to create a "Black public sphere," which included a public space of her own, to argue issues.[18]

Shadd Cary, who became a leader in the emigration movement, lectured in halls while securing subscriptions to the newspaper.

She had to pretend that she was not the sole editor. She was eventually ousted from the newspaper in 1855 after she used her own name, along with the name of her assistant editor and sister, in the masthead; the community's Black male leadership were not pleased. But she had made her point, becoming the first Black woman to edit a newspaper on the continent. She made a statement that echoed to Wells' generation: "To Colored women, we have a word—we have 'broken the Editorial ice,' whether willingly or not, for your class in America; so go to editing, as many of you that are willing, and as soon as you may, if you think you are ready."[19]

Black Media Ideology

Ida B. Wells, like Shadd Cary, was about to test the power of the press from her own Black perspective.

In my doctoral dissertation on Black mass media ideology, I said:

I have defined Black media as Black-owned and/or Black-oriented transmission of Black media experiences; they serve to reflect and reinforce an African-American identity outside of white political, social, economic, cultural and spiritual hegemony. Black media create connections—exchanges of ideas and information—that lead to the development of a collective, albeit varied, political, social, economic, cultural and spiritual consciousness. Black media, then, becomes a communal experience, where Blacks speak in their own voices to themselves in their own collective space....

The history of Black media is the history of committed activists and/or community workers who, in various ways, use media in an attempt to answer the following three questions for themselves and their audiences. First, how do Blacks survive and thrive as a people? Second, how do Blacks resist white supremacy? Third, how do Blacks organize to save themselves and, by extension, the rest of society?

To these activists, working in media is an honored profession, but even more so it is just one of many activities they have used to further the cause of racial and social justice in America; it is a way to engage in collective public struggle outside and against white hegemony. It has also been a way for Black activists over the decades to seize control over their personal destinies, allowing them, in turn, to use their vehicles to push other Blacks to control their collective destiny....[20]

Later on I wrote:

In the beginning, the Black press served as offense and defense. It began both as a response to white media supremacy and the vehicle for free African-Americans to see

> their own words. The heart of African communication—the drum and the word *(nommo)* the voices of the village—met the technology of the European-created printed press with empowering results.[21]

Bennett wrote that the creation of periodicals allowed for different colonies of Black America "[to] co-exist in the same time zone" and "brought the Black community together and focused its thinking."[22]

Still later on I wrote:

> The Black press of the nineteenth century began articulating the themes that would propel it into the twenty-first century: 1) freedom, 2) self-determination and 3) social and political equality for African-Americans.....Written and published words, in the hands of free African-Americans, were forged into human rights documents demanding emancipation. Journalism was just a part of an evangelical-like mission to fight

white supremacy and secure Black self-determination.....From slavery to emancipation to the decades of Jim Crow, these activist-publishers used their platforms to argue for, respectively, liberation, emigration and an end to white racism's most violent manifestations. Their words inspired freedom. Their decisions to be advocacy journalists, as full-time paid professionals, gave them individual self-determination, which allowed for them to freely fight for the equality and self-determination articulated by the U.S. Constitution. Such independence meant being able to articulate Black reality, explaining it to friends and foes alike.[23]

Iola's Free Speech And Its Consequences

Wells moved from teaching to full-time journalism when she became editor and co-owner of *The Free Speech*. For the strong, independent Wells, it was just a change in vocation. Like Shadd Cary, she traveled, speaking and selling subscriptions.

She advocated self-help in her columns. Wells also encouraged Blacks to stand up for themselves. In 1892, she cheered Blacks in Atlanta for boycotting Jim Crow streetcars. Using her pen name, "Iola," she wrote:

> Let the Afro-American depend on no party, but on himself, for his salvation. Let him continue to get education, character, and above all, put money in his purse. When he has a dollar in his pocket and many more in the bank, he can move from injustice and oppression and no one can say him nay. When he has money, and plenty of it, parties and races will become his servants.[24]

One of Wells' biographers, Linda O. McMurray, has written that Wells' early newspaper writings reflect her struggles for class, gender, political and racial identity.[25] Like Douglass and Shadd Cary before her, she used journalism not only to figure out a role for herself and her people, but to speak out on any injustice. "Her pen became her tool for confronting much of what angered her...Journalism was also the medium through which she eventually defined herself."[26]

Wells enjoyed and appreciated the impact her work was having among her people. The editor herself wrote that "every week evidence came from all over Mississippi, Tennessee, and Arkansas that *The Free Speech* was a welcome visitor, a helpful influence in the lives of our people, and was filling a long-felt want."[27]

Wells showed both her religious devotion and courage when she again used her forum to root out all injustices. She made enemies with her words, but also made sure those words were consistent with her dedication to truth. She recalled:

> Several incidents happened to illustrate that influence. A minister of the gospel who had gone from his church services one Sunday night

to the home of one of the members, who was a grass widow, had been surprised by her husband, who not only ran him out the house in his night clothes but took possession of the new broadcloth suit which the sisters had given him, and also his shoes and hat. The husband was an expressman, and he nailed Rev. ——-'s shoes to the front of his express wagon and the hat to the rear, and drove around town exhibiting them in the performance of his duties the next week.

The minister remained in hiding until a brother minister could furnish him some clothing and money with which to get out of town. Of which *The Free Speech* had a very caustic comment on this particular incident and that type of minister. The preacher's alliance at its meeting the following Monday morning voted to boycott *The Free Speech* because of that comment and exposure of that incident. They sent the presiding elder of the district to the office to threaten us with the loss of their patronage and the fight they were going to make against us in their congregations.

We answered this threat by publishing the names of every minister who belonged to the alliance in the next issue of *The Free Speech,* and told the community that these men upheld the immoral conduct of one of their number and asked if they were willing to support preachers who would sneak into their homes when their backs were turned and debauch their wives. Needless to say we never heard any more about the boycott, and *The Free Speech* flourished like a green bay tree.[28]

It did flourish—until Tommie Moss, a friend of Wells, one of a trio of Black businessmen who were lynched in 1892 because they threatened white economic power in Memphis.

The story:

On March 2, Black and white children playing marbles got into a fight near The People's Grocery, a place where Moss worked with manager Calvin McDowell and clerk Will "Henry" Stewart. The white boy's father came out to beat up the Black child, Armour Harris. The three Black men left their store to defend Harris. William Barrett, a white business competitor of the three Black men, got hit—bludgeoned—near the People's Grocery. Barrett, bringing the police, came back to the scene the next day, and accused Stewart as being his attacker. McDowell, who came to the door, was struck by the police officer when he said that Stewart was not there. McDowell was hit by a revolver, which hit the ground. He got up, picked it up, and shot at Barrett. McDowell was arrested and released, but the police issued a warrant for both Harris, the child, and Stewart. The Black community where the store resided met and pledged to clean out the "damned white trash" (Barrett and his store). Barrett told the authorities that Blacks were conspiring against whites. A

Black painter getting shot by a clerk in a separate white store was enough to galvanize the Black neighborhood into action. When six armed white men, many deputized, began to raid the People's Grocery, the Black residents shot back. Following the shootout, hundreds of whites were deputized to put the Black community in its place. Forty Blacks were arrested, including Harris, his mother, and Moss. After a few days of being held in jail, a white mob appeared, and lynched McDowell, Moss and Stewart. Moss allegedly said as his last words: "Tell my people to go West. There is no justice for them here."[29] The mob shot any Blacks in front of the People's Grocery, and then raided and destroyed it. What was left of it was sold to Barrett.

Wrote Ida: "Tom Moss was as fine a man that ever walked the streets of Memphis...yet he was murdered with no more consideration than if he had been a dog, because he as a man defended his property from attack. The colored people feel that every white man in Memphis who consented to his death is as guilty as those who fired the guns which took his life, and they want to get away from this town."[30]

Wells, enraged, called for Blacks to leave Memphis in protest. She wrote in her newspaper:

> The city of Memphis has demonstrated that neither character nor standing avails the Negro if he dares to protect himself against the white man or become his rival. There is nothing we can do about the lynching now, as we are outnumbered and without arms. The white mob could help itself to ammunition without pay, but the order was rigidly enforced against the selling of guns to Negroes. There is therefore only one thing left we can do; save our money and leave a town which will neither protect our lives and our property, nor give us a fair trial in the courts, but takes us out and murders us in cold blood when accused by white persons.[31]

And they left, by the hundreds, heading West to Oklahoma and other states.

Wells continued to editorialize about lynching—a crime usually accompanied by a charge that the lynching victim, usually a Black male, had raped a white woman. When Wells wrote a *Free Speech* editorial saying that perhaps attractions between white women and Black men were more complex and voluntary than that—a conclusion white men did not want to reach—her presses were destroyed by a white Memphis mob when Wells was away. The obsession white men had with their notions of chivalry—which did not apply to the Black women they would act out their sexual desires with, voluntary or not—had led to white mob violence.

Arriving in New York when she heard the news about *The Free Speech*, she was hired by T. Thomas Fortune, publisher of *The New York Age,* a leading Black newspaper there.

Wells had decided to publish what she knew about lynchings. In June of 1892,

Fortune published her first findings—bylined "Exiled"—on *The Age's* front page.[32]

It was the beginning of Wells' travels around the country and in Europe, writing and speaking on the evils of lynching. The former teacher had found a large classroom to instruct on how to use words for liberating purposes. Like Douglass, Walker and Shadd Cary, Wells' vocation had found her, and her journalistic role now would be a permanent one in Black America.

CHAPTER FOUR
Knotted Rope: Wells' Campaigns Against Lynching

It starts with the actions of a small white mob, and ends with a somewhat large white community celebration.

The white mob goes to the courthouse to look for the Black accused. The local authorities either look the other way or join in as the crowd takes the victim. The Black victim is almost always male and the lynching is almost always in the South.

A small group of white men take the Black victim to a field with a large, strong tree. A white crowd—of all ages, mind you—gathers around. After all, it is the day's, or week's, or month's entertainment in that town.

The small group takes a rope and ties it around the victim's neck. With the white crowd swelling in size and excitement, it then throws the rope over the tree branch.

The victim is strung up on the tree, gurgling for life until he suffocates. Or until his neck breaks.

His pants are pulled down. His manhood is sliced off, and then stuffed into his mouth.

Then the Black body is set on fire.

The white crowd swells, and begins to cheer. The publicly-sanctioned, illegal execution of a Black man has become a carnival.

The flames produce hot color into the air.

If a camera is available, pictures are taken. The crowd poses, sometimes behind the body.

Later, in some cases, postcards are even made and sold.

Souvenirs could include the postcards or the Black man's internal or external organs.

Members of the white "moderate" community—filled with elected officials, business leaders, and other leading citizens, people who consider themselves morally good and well-meaning—ignore the incident. Unless they are participating in it.

The white religious community, teaching from the Ten Commandments every Sunday *("Thou Shall Not Kill")*, ignores the incident—or *defends* it.

White newspapers, however, write about the incident, but do not editorialize against it. They defend it also.

The Black body stays there for several days, for all to see. The public price of standing up to white supremacy, in the form of that charred, sexually mutilated carcass, was on extended display, in county after county, state after state, decade after decade.

From 1865 to 1965 (if you count the murders of Emmett Till in 1955 and, in 1964, of civil rights activists James Chaney, Andrew Goodman and Michael "Mickey" Schwerner, the latter two white) this was done to a Black person by a white mob an estimated 4,000 times over a century.

There was no justice for the victims. No one was ever punished in any way.

There were no legal or government redresses. Local and state governments, all white, either passed anti-lynching laws that they didn't enforce, and/or looked the other way. The three branches of the federal government, regardless of party, were permanently silent while violent, unsanctioned murder was committed repeatedly in America. From time to time, anti-lynching bills were discussed, and sometimes drafted into legislation, but, championless, they littered the floors of Congress. There was no presidential statement about the South's murder-in-the-shadows until the Civil Rights Movement sped up in the 1960s.

The clear majority of the families of the victims did not receive any reparations—not even to this day.

This is the Jim Crow America in which Ida B. Wells-Barnett spent her entire life.

—§—

It is not properly emphasized in American history that the system of Jim Crow was not just a set of public customs that required separate water fountains and bathrooms; it was more wide-ranging, and more evil, than that. Segregation was a comprehensive, dehumanizing social arrangement for Blacks, and it was constantly reinforced by a century of arbitrary, brutal violence decided by, and executed by, racist whites. Terror was used by whites to keep Blacks in line, in their collective place. Black men could be lynched at any time for any supposed offense before, and without, a trial, and Black women could be raped by white men with impunity. Blacks could not only not count on American justice, *they were not even in control of their own bodies.*[33] Jim Crow, then, was an extension of slavery, since it was structured to keep white social control intact through fear of violent consequence. So even the *idea* of publicly challenging any of this in any way was quickly scuttled, because it risked an instant, vicious death by the white mob and the possible rape of a female family member.

Wells, who had to escape a Memphis lynch mob because she dared to utilize the free speech right of the First Amendment of the United States Constitution, was also a great believer in the amendment that immediately followed—the Second, the one allowing armed self-defense. She carried a gun on her person. She wrote in her 1892 pamphlet, *Southern Horrors: Lynch Law in all its Phases*, that "the Winchester rifle deserved a place of honor in every Black home and it should be used for that protection which the law refuses to give. When the white man who is always the aggressor knows he runs as great risk of biting the dust every time his Afro-American victim does, he will have greater respect for Afro-American life. The more the Afro-American yields and cringes and begs, the more he has to do so, the more he is insulted, outraged and lynched."[34]

But Wells, as courageous as she was—as many Blacks in her time could be and were, since there were scattered incidents in the late nineteenth and early twentieth century of Blacks defending their land by gunfire—could not fight Southern white lynch mobs who had societal backing because of white supremacy. She could not kill those white men who had lynched Tommie Moss, Calvin McDowell and Will "Henry" Stewart, nor could she violently avenge any of the other Black victims she would write about for decades. She could not even help bring any of the lynchers to justice, anywhere. But she could investigate and document the crimes.

In her early years of this work, she often felt abandoned by Black (male) leadership. "[T]he obstacles to Wells' support were not only the intimidating specter of violence or the opinion that her confrontational methods created more problems than they solved," wrote Giddings. "Her campaign forced Blacks of means and influence to face—or face down—the existential quality of their lives."[35]

As Ida B. Wells, she travelled the United States and Europe, explaining constantly that lynching proved that America was not a nation of laws when it came to Black people. As Ida B. Wells-Barnett, she was repeatedly pulled from her family and her community work in Chicago to investigate a lynching somewhere in the land of the free.

—§—

The following is a select timeline of Ida B. Wells' anti-lynching work.

1892

Living in exile in New York City, Wells writes an extended expose, "The Truth About Lynching," that is run in seven columns on the front page of *The New York Age*. The article is later that year republished in pamphlet form as *Southern Horrors: Lynch Law in all its Phases*. In that pamphlet, she recounted several examples of consensual relationships between Black men and white women in Memphis, Mississippi, and false rape charges in Mississippi, Texas and elsewhere. Repeatedly, using clippings of well-known stories from established white newspapers, Wells showed the power that the word of white women of any class distinction had over the life of any type of Black man. She also discusses that in many of these cases, it was the city's foremost residents that were directly (or indirectly, through indifference or to provide excuse) part of these lynch mobs. She also listed incidents of the rape of Black women by white males and even the lynching of Black women for accused crimes. Using statistics from major white newspapers, she showed that the constant white charges of Black rape didn't match the actual numbers. This pamphlet showed that what was at risk was not the honor or white womanhood, but the power white men—many of whom Wells added, ironically, had a sexual obsession with Black women—had and exercised in subjugating its Black population. "Wells made the miscegenation [sexual race-mixing] at the hands of whites not simply a complaint but evidence that it was part and parcel of the larger race issue that was also informed by gender and sexuality," wrote Giddings.[36]

1893

Wells, through her hiring of detectives, investigated the lynching of Henry Smith, a man with mental illness who had been accused of murdering a four-year-old girl in Paris, Texas. She was the daughter of the town's sheriff. After his capture, Smith—whom Wells did not say was innocent—was subjected to being burnt all over his body by iron pokers that were red-hot. His eyes were burnt out and the burning rods were put down his throat. He was then doused in kerosene and set afire. In addition to the crowd being entertained, whites found more ways of using his Black body's agony. His screams were recorded by gramophone and sold. A pamphlet was published about the case—from a *pro*-lynching standpoint—and sold.

Wells, abolitionist luminary Fredrick Douglass and writer/teacher I. Garland Penn publish *The Reason The Colored American Is Not in the World's Columbian Exposition: The Afro-American's Contribution to Columbian Literature*, a pamphlet for the occasion of "Jubilee Day," a day set aside for Blacks, at the World's Columbian Exposition, a world's fair in Chicago celebrating the 400th anniversary of Columbus' trip to the New World. Wells—who reluctantly agreed to this idea because of her respect for Douglass, who was set to speak that day—wrote most of the pamphlet, including the chapter "Lynch Law." This is part of her introduction:

> This law continues in force to-day in some of the oldest states of the Union, where courts of justice have long been established, whose laws are executed by white Americans. It flourishes most largely in the states which foster the convict lease system, and is brought to bear mainly, against the Negro. The first fifteen years of his freedom he was murdered by masked mobs for trying to vote. Public opinion having made lynching for that cause unpopular, a new reason is given to justify the murders of the

past 15 years. The Negro was first charged with attempting to rule white people, and hundreds were murdered on that pretended supposition. He is now charged with assaulting or attempting to assault white women. This charge, as false as it is foul, robs us of the sympathy of the world and is blasting the race's good name.

The men who make these charges encourage or lead the mobs which do the lynching. They belong to the race which holds Negro life cheap, which owns the telegraph wires, newspapers, and all other communication with the outside world. They write the reports which justify lynching by painting the Negro as Black as possible, and those reports are accepted by the press associations and the world without question or investigation. The mob spirit had increased with alarming frequency and violence. Over a thousand Black men, women and children have been thus sacrificed the past ten years. Masks have long since been thrown aside and the lynchings of the present day take place in broad daylight. The sheriffs, police, and state officials stand by and see the work done well. The coroner's jury is often formed among those who took part in the lynching and a verdict, "Death at the hands of parties unknown to the jury" is rendered. As the number of lynchings have increased, so has the cruelty and barbarism of the lynchers. Three human beings were burned alive in civilized America during the first six months of this year (1893). Over one hundred have been lynched in this half year. They were hanged, then cut, shot and burned.[37]

She then laid out the statistics and lynching accounts from newspapers such as, respectively, *The Chicago Tribune* and *The Memphis Commercial, The Chicago Inter-*

Ocean and *The* (Memphis, Tennessee) *Public Ledger*.

Wells goes undercover as the widow of C.J. Miller, accused of murdering two white girls, with him raping and slitting the throat of one. Wells was asked by *The Chicago Inter-Ocean* to investigate. The newspaper published her report on the front page and in six columns. Miller had an alibi of where he was on the day of the murder. After he was killed, it was established that he was not in Bardwell, Kentucky, where the murder took place. The real alleged killer, a white farmer in a nearby section of Missouri, was found by a bloodhound. What made it worse that a witness describes a man he had seen going to Missouri around the time of the crime was either a light-skinned mulatto or a white man. Miller's brown-skinned body had had its fingers and toes slashed off and set afire. Wells wrote that this murder happened "in the glare of the nineteenth century civilization by those who profess to believe in Christianity, law and order."[38]

1894

The London Anti-Lynching Committee, created after Wells spoke there, comes to America to investigate the murder of six Black men in Kerrville, Tennessee. The six men were arrested for burning down a white man's farm after years of conflicts between Blacks and whites there. The men, manacled and on a train, were gunned down by a white mob who, somehow, knew the route the train was taking. The British coming armed with facts made Tennessee officials move publicly. The governor, Peter Turney, announced a $5,000 reward, and *The Commercial Appeal* editorialized against the lynchers after talking about how Blacks commit crimes.[39]

1895

Wells public campaign had indeed increased national awareness about lynching. Anti-lynching laws had been passed in North Carolina and Georgia, and, in 1895, South Carolina. (More states—Kentucky,

Texas and Ohio—would follow in 1897). She published *A Red Record*, her most extensive anti-lynching pamphlet to date. She updated the lynching statistics and named victims. An excerpt of the introduction, titled "The Case Stated":

> The Negro has suffered much and is willing to suffer more. He recognizes that the wrongs of two centuries can not be righted in a day, and he tries to bear his burden with patience for today and be hopeful for tomorrow.
>
> But there comes a time when the veriest worm will turn, and the Negro feels today that after all the work he has done, all the sacrifices he has made, and all the suffering he has endured, if he did not, now, defend his name and manhood from this vile accusation, he would be unworthy even of the contempt of mankind. It is to this charge he now feels he must make answer.

If the Southern people in defense of their lawlessness, would tell the truth and admit that colored men and women are lynched for almost any offense, from murder to a misdemeanor, there would not now be the necessity for this defense. But when they intentionally, maliciously and constantly belie the record and bolster up these falsehoods by the words of legislators, preachers, governors and bishops, then the Negro must give to the world his side of the awful story.[40]

1897

The lynching of Charles "Chick" Mitchell, a Black milkman who delivered cream to the widow of a newspaper publisher, was the first test of that state's anti-lynching law. The test didn't happen, because the legislation was stalled in court.

1898

Frazier Baker, the first Black postmaster in Lake City, South Carolina, was lynched because he refused to resign his position. He was boycotted by the town, and had to move the post office to his house because the building was set afire. Baker was shot by a mob who had surrounded his house. It was burned down, and his one-year old baby daughter was fatally shot. Four other children were shot in the groin, abdomen, right hand and left elbow. Blacks demanded federal action. Both Barnetts—Ida and her husband Ferdinand—spoke at a mass meeting. Wells-Barnett was part of a delegation that went to Washington to demand reparations for the Baker family. She directly challenged President McKinley to do something about this case. Congress debated reparation bills for the family, but the legislation was forgotten when the U.S.S. Maine in Havana was blown up, the spark that started the Spanish-American War. Fifteen Lake City citizens were indicted, however, by the Justice Department.

When a white mob took over Wilmington, North Carolina, stripping the Blacks of all their positions, Wells-Barnett attacked President McKinley for inaction: "[McKinley was] too much interested....in the national decoration of [C]onfederate graves to pay any attention to the Negro's rights," she said at a Afro-American Council meeting.[41] A delegation of the Council got to meet with McKinley, but Wells-Barnett was persuaded not to attend.

1899

Samuel Wilkes, also known as Sam Hose, was lynched in Palmetto, Georgia. Blacks had been arrested for setting fire to several blocks. A white mob broke into a warehouse where authorities were holding the men. They shot them. Later, a body of a white farmer was found in Palmetto. Hose was suspected because he had worked for the farmer. He was accused of killing the farmer, raping his wife twice, and throwing their baby to the floor. When he was caught, he was tied to a tree. Parts of his body, including his genitals, were cut off and he was set afire. Wells-Barnett was so incensed, she wrote an entire pamphlet on the case, called *Lynch Law in Georgia*. The pamphlet also carried the comments of Louis Le Vin, a Chicago detective that Wells fundraised for and hired to investigate the case. Le Vin found that Wilkes and Cranford had argued over wages. At one point, Cranford pulled out a gun, and Wilkes had thrown an ax at Cranford in self-defense. The detective said Wilkes did not confess to harming Cranford's wife and child, and did not plea for mercy when being mutilated.[42]

Wells-Barnett wrote:

> The real purpose of these savage demonstrations is to teach the Negro that in the South he has no rights that the law will enforce. Samuel Hose was burned to teach the Negroes that no matter what a white man does to them, they must

> not resist. Hose, a servant, had killed Cranford, his employer. An example must be made. Ordinary punishment was deemed inadequate. This Negro must be burned alive. To make the burning a certainty the charge of outrage was invented, and added to the charge of murder. The daily press offered reward for the capture of Hose and then openly incited the people to burn him as soon as caught. The mob carried out the plan in every savage detail.[43]

This time, Wells-Barnett traded in statistics for passionate narrative. She detailed every lynching that she had listed in that pamphlet, and in dramatic detail. She returned the pamphlet's second chapter to Hose, titled "Tortured and Burned Alive."

> The burning of Samuel Hose, or, to give his right name, Samuel Wilkes, gave to the United States the distinction of having burned alive seven human beings during

the past ten years. The details of this deed of unspeakable barbarism have shocked the civilized world, for it is conceded universally that no other nation on earth, civilized or savage, has put to death any human being with such atrocious cruelty as that inflicted upon Samuel Hose by the Christian white people of Georgia.

The charge is generally made that lynch law is condemned by the best white people of the South, and that lynching is the work of the lowest and lawless class. Those who seek the truth know the fact to be, that all classes are equally guilty, for what the one class does the other encourages, excuses and condones.

This was clearly shown in the burning of Hose. This awful deed was suggested, encouraged and made possible by the daily press of Atlanta, Georgia, until the burning actually occurred, and then it immediately condoned the burning by a hysterical plea to "consider the facts."[44]

1900

Wells-Barnett wrote an article, "Lynch Law in America," for the Boston *Arena*. She also wrote a pamphlet, *Mob Rule in New Orleans*, about the police murder of Robert Charles, who refused to turn himself in and blame himself for police harassment. He defended himself against the authorities with a Winchester rifle. Wells-Barnett defended his honor and praised his bravery against white racist police officers:

> In any law-abiding community Charles would have been justified in delivering himself up immediately to the properly constituted authorities and asking a trial by a jury of his peers. He could have been certain that in resisting an unwarranted arrest he had a right

to defend his life, even to the point of taking one in that defense, but Charles knew that his arrest in New Orleans, even for defending his life, meant nothing short of a long term in the penitentiary, and still more probable death by lynching at the hands of a cowardly mob. He very bravely determined to protect his life as long as he had breath in his body and strength to draw a hair trigger on his would-be murderers.[45]

1909

The lynching of William "Frog" James for the murder of a young white girl in Cairo, Illinois—whose body was found nude—was a test of the state's anti-lynching law and a significant, direct victory for Wells-Barnett. A first Black male suspect was released by police. James was arrested and was taken to a small town. But the lynch mob took no chances on James. They brought him back to Cairo, threw a rope around his neck, and strung him up in the center of town. Hundreds of whites had gathered, and when the rope broke, the crowd fired into James. His body was set on fire, and his internal organs gutted for later sale as souvenirs. Supposedly James implicated another Black man, but when the mob couldn't find him, they lynched a white male prisoner, Henry Saltzner. The sheriff was implicated in allowing the mob to kill James, and Wells-Barnett went to Cairo to investigate. She pushed local, highly reluctant Blacks to sign a resolution saying the sheriff had failed to protect James. She presented her case in court in Springfield. The governor publicly announced that the sheriff would not be keeping his job.

1910

Wells-Barnett became directly involved in trying to stop the extradition from Chicago to Arkansas of Steve Green, a Black man who had killed the white man he had been working for because the white man shot him for working in another farm in another state. The newly-created NAACP gets involved, and Wells-Barnett, referred to by NAACP officials as a Chicago association representative, took Green to Canada. He then returned to Chicago, and the authorities retracted the extradition order. The Association publicly congratulated itself on Green's rescue in the first issue of *The Crisis* magazine, the association's organ, but refuses to mention Wells-Barnett by name.[46]

1915

Wells-Barnett gets involved in the case of Joe Campbell, a Black prisoner (for killing a labor member) who was now in solitary because he had been accused of killing the wife of the warden. He was made to confess to the crime, then recanted. Ferdinand Barnett, Ida's husband, agreed to defend him. He was sentenced to life in prison in 1918.

1917

Wells-Barnett traveled to East St. Louis to investigate a major riot. Black men, defending themselves, shot at a car filled with white men brandishing revolvers and cursing and yelling. Police arrived, but not in uniform and driving the same type of car as the white disrupters. Shots were fired from the Black community, and two white detectives were fatally shot. Whites marched in the next day and terrorized the Black community—killing, setting homes on fire, and other destruction. At least 30 Blacks were killed and two hundred homes were burned down. Wells-Barnett called a meeting of her Negro Fellowship League, and her husband, speaking there, told his audience to arm themselves.[47] Wells-Barnett's pamphlet was called *The East St. Louis Massacre: The Greatest Outrage of the Century*. It gave a first-person account of her stories and some of the victims she had met, as well as accounts from major newspapers.

An excerpt:

All the impartial witnesses agree that the police were either indifferent or encouraged the barbarities, and that the major part of the National Guard was indifferent or inactive. No organized effort was made to protect the Negroes or disperse the murdering groups. The lack of frenzy and of a large infuriated mob made the task easy. Ten determined officers could have prevented most of the outrages. One hundred men acting with authority and vigor might have prevented any outrage.

The stain cannot be wiped from the record of Illinois, but the State may be vindicated by punishment of the officers responsible for the conduct of the guardsmen; and by the vigorous prosecution of the murder leaders.

East St. Louisans have a duty to perform in looking into the conduct of their own city government, which permitted the trouble to culminate in these atrocities. They should find out the cause of the fatal weakness which encouraged the race riots and paralyzed the police while innocent men, women and children were shot, burned and tortured. The future of the city which in point of growth and prosperity is a marvel, should prompt thorough action by law-abiding citizens.[48]

Wells-Barnett is involved in the case of Black soldiers who are facing stiff and disproportionate sentences for mutiny. (Le Roy Bundy, a Black man who whites had accused of shooting into the white officer's car in East St. Louis, was somehow made the scapegoat for this case. He was threatened with the death penalty, and eventually took a plea bargain. Wells-Barnett interviewed him for *The Chicago Defender*. He was sentenced to life in 1919.) Thirteen of the soldiers were hanged. Eleven more were given a death sentence. Wells-Barnett also interviewed them for *The Defender*. She wore buttons made about the soldiers. She was interrogated by two federal intelligence officers about it, and threatened with the charge of treason. She refused to be intimidated by them. An intelligence report was written about the encounter, and it was added to the Barnetts' growing file.[49]

1919

Hyde Park, a white Chicago neighborhood, now had new Black neighbors. In response, 14 bombs targeted families or realtors. (The Barnetts had purchased a home there.) Wells-Barnett organized the Black community and wrote about the situation for *The Chicago Tribune*, but the issue gets supplanted by the Chicago riot. It started as a rock-throwing fight between Black and white teens over a beach. A white man threw a rock at the Black boys, killing one of them. The police refused to arrest him. A group of Blacks assaulted the white policeman who refused to arrest that white rock-thrower. The riots continued for seven days. In *The Chicago Tribune,* Wells-Barnett, complaining that the police only searched Black homes for weapons, defended the right of Blacks to defend themselves. She attempted to do some organizing, but was stymied by NAACP Assistant National Secretary Walter White.

Wells-Barnett tried to get support for the Blacks accused in what became known as the Elaine, Arkansas massacre. Whites had killed Blacks there because they had heard of a Black conspiracy to kill whites. This charge was not true; what really happened was that union officials were trying to organize the Black sharecroppers. Wells-Barnett, still writing for the growing *Chicago Defender,* had competed with the NAACP for leadership over this conflict. The following year, she published a major pamphlet, *The Arkansas Race Riot*, her largest, documenting the riots and the subsequent trial of the Black men arrested.

She wrote:

> The colored farmers combined, counseled together, employed counsel to present their plea. They did

not threaten to strike, did not strike, menaced nothing, injured nobody, and yet:

Hundreds of them today are penniless, "Refugees from pillaged homes";

More than a hundred were killed by white mobs, for which not one white man has been arrested;

Seventy-five men are serving life sentences in the penitentiary, and

Twelve men are sentenced to die.

If this is democracy, what is bolshevism?[50]

1920

U.S. Rep. Leonidas Dyer, a Republican from St. Louis, reintroduces an anti-lynching bill in the House of Representatives. It would eventually pass the House two years later, but die in the Senate.

—§—

The cause that Wells-Barnett poured her lifetime into would be fought by others after her death.

The NAACP would continue its anti-lynching campaigns well into the 1940s.

Eleanor Roosevelt, the wife of President Franklin Delano Roosevelt, was trying to assist the NAACP's Walter White in pushing the president forward. The First Lady would cajole her husband to fight for the passage of anti-lynching bills in Congress, but the president didn't want his New Deal legislation to be stopped by Southern Democrats, known as "Dixiecrats."

In the end, only two things stopped lynching *en masse*:

1. The fact that modern society—with constant mass mobilizations for civil rights and a modern mass communications media, notably television and radio—took lynching out of the shadows of Southern "customs" and into the national, and international, spotlight. By the 1950s, it was no longer an easy task to hide

the mob violence in an isolated field or small public square. Racial violence now got national and international attention in hundreds of newspapers and over the local and national airwaves, which produced massive national and local political pressure, which, in turn, produced some sort of result.

2. That when Black people in the South got the right to vote, they got to elect police and other officials who were accountable to their communities.

Community mobilizing, accountability and media. Those three acorns—like Wells-Barnett, hard to crack but full of power and promise—could be traced back to her campaigns. After a century of much ink, paper and blood, all with limited success, they were successfully planted in Black America in the mid-twentieth century, and the beautiful, enormous trees that grew from them knew no ropes, no strange fruit, no white-racist postcard poses.

CHAPTER FIVE
The "Princess of the Press" Becomes a Feted Clubwoman

In 1892, Ida B. Wells adjusted as well she could to New York, to her new life in the North without her family, without her Memphis community, without *The Free Speech*, her "Iola" pen name or the "Princess of the Press" nickname her writings had wrought. Always undaunted, never depressed or defeated, she began to speak about her experience at the city's Black literary clubs.

Her work speaking, and her introduction to various members of the Black community through her writing and Fortune, led her to meet several Black women activists, including: Sarah Garnet, the daughter of abolitionist Henry Highland Garnet and the New York's first Black school principal; her sister, Susan Smith McKinney, the first woman to gain a license to practice medicine in the state, and Victoria Earle Matthews, a fellow Black journalist.

Matthews suggested having an event in Wells' honor that would double as a fundraiser to turn her article into a pamphlet. They wanted Black women from the East Coast—Philadelphia, Boston—as well as those in Manhattan and Brooklyn–to take part. A committee of 250 women formed to organize the testimonial, which was going to be held in Lyric Hall in Manhattan. She spoke forcefully about what had been done to her friends, tears flowing from her eyes. The event raised $400, and the *Age* article she had written turned into the pamphlet *Southern Horrors*.

Out of this October 1892 event came the creation of two Black women's clubs—The Woman's Era Club and the and the Women's Loyal Union. The latter was led by Matthews, while the former was headed by Josephine Ruffin in Boston. In her autobiography, Wells wrote that that event "was the real beginning of the club movement among the colored women in this country."[51]

Black women's civic and political clubs performed important social and political work in the Black communities for decades. Rosalyn Terborg-Penn, professor emerita of history at Morgan State University, an historically Black institution, describes Black women's clubs thusly in her seminal work, *African American Women in the Struggle for the Vote, 1850-1920:*

> Hundreds of Black women's clubs mobilized for the vote during the years 1900 to 1920. Some were independent clubs formed in churches and in neighborhoods to aid the community. Others were affiliated with national organizations such as the Baptist Women's Convention and the NACW [the National Association of Colored Women], often through state federations. Still others were secret societies such as sororities of college women and their alumnae, or women's auxil-

iaries of Masonic orders. In addition, there were a small number of organized trade union women and even some Black women's suffrage clubs. Collectively and singularly, each developed the appropriate strategies for gaining the ballot, or in states where women could vote, for electing the candidates of their choice.[52]

The newly-formed clubwomen were not the only residents of Black America praising Wells. Frederick Douglass, who had met her at a colored press association meeting in 1889, wrote the following about her in a 1892 *New York Age* editorial:

> Let me give you thanks for your faithful paper on the lynch abomination now generally practiced against colored people in the South. There has been no word equal to it in convincing power. I have spoken, but my word is feeble in com-

parison. You give us what you know and testify from actual knowledge. You have dealt with the facts with cool, painstaking fidelity and left those naked and uncontradicted facts to speak for themselves.

Brave woman! You have done your people and mine a service which can neither be weighed nor measured. If American conscience were only half alive, if the American church and clergy were only half christianized, if American moral sensibility were not hardened by persistent infliction of outrage and crime against colored people, a scream of horror, shame and indignation would rise to Heaven wherever your pamphlet shall be read.

But alas! Even crime has power to reproduce itself and create conditions favorable to its own existence. It sometimes seems we are deserted by earth and Heaven yet we must still think, speak and work, and trust in the power of a merciful God for final deliverance.[53]

Very truly and gratefully yours,
FREDERICK DOUGLASS
Cedar Hill, Anacostia, D.C., Oct. 25, 1892

This full-throated endorsement by Douglass would be somewhat tempered later, as is discussed in Chapter 8, when Wells would become more international in scope. She would travel to England twice, and those trips would result in the creation of the London Anti-Lynching Committee.

—§—

Wells would be involved in Black women's clubs, in one way or another, for the rest of her life. As Ida B. Wells-Barnett, in 1896 she would help found the National Association of Colored Women, a group that exists in the twenty-first century.[54] The NACW was founded by a merger between the National Federation of Afro-American Women, a group just founded the year before, and the National League of Colored Women. Wells-Barnett was a leader of the fused group. When living abolitionist legend Harriet Tubman raised the infant Charles Barnett, Ida's first-born son, over her head to the assembled activists, Giddings wrote that "it was the last time Ida would feel so close to the organization—the first national secular Black women's group ever created—that her efforts had been so instrumental in spawning."[55] Conservative winds were blowing from Tuskegee, Alabama, and would decisively shape Black America's two decades.

—§—

One of the more notable clubs Wells-Barnett was involved in during her organizing years in Chicago was her Alpha Suffrage Club. It was a major part of the get-out-the-vote efforts in Black Chicago in 1914, the year women in Illinois gained the right to vote. (Because Blacks could vote in the North, states which enfranchised women by law included Black women.) Wells-Barnett wrote about the opposition it got—from sexist Black men and reluctant Black women:

> The women who joined were extremely interested when I showed them that we could use our vote for the advantage of ourselves and our race. We organized the block system, and once a week we met to report progress. The women at first were very much discouraged.
>
> They said the men jeered at them and told them they ought to be at home taking care of the babies. Others insisted that the women were trying to take the place of men and wear the trousers. I urged each one of the workers to go back and tell the women that we wanted them [men and women] to register so that they could help put a colored *man* on the City Council.
>
> This line of argument appealed very strongly to them, since we had already taken part in several campaigns where men had run inde-

pendently for alderman. The work of these women was so effective that when registration day came, the Second Ward was the sixth highest of the thirty-five wards of the city.[56]

Along with Mary Church Terrell and other leading Black women of the late nineteenth and early twentieth centuries, Ida B. Wells would be associated with Black clubwomen; so much so, that in Chicago, the Ida B. Wells Club was formed in 1893. Giddings wrote that by February 1894, there were more than 300 members.[57]

CHAPTER SIX
Ida's Alphabet: NAACP, NACW, NFL, NERL

The faith Ida B. Wells-Barnett had in organizations sadly was not reciprocal. Except for the brief, freelance-activist period between Memphis and Chicago, she had always been part of a community unit of some type that did some daily work: a school, a newspaper. She always would.

Creating a new life for her in Chicago meant a continuation of the kind of collective effort she had made all her life. With her new roles of wife and mother established, and with a new newspaper, *The Conservator*, she set out to make positive changes in national, state and local African-American life while consistently defending both the honor of African-American women and the bodies of both Black men and women.

In her organizational battles over several decades, she had true allies—most notably, the activist and fellow newspaper editor William Monroe Trotter—but she had to deal with many of those fellow travelers who felt she was too outspoken, too militant, too nonconformist. Wells-Barnett lived in the historical shadow between the abolitionist Frederick Douglass and the accomodationist leader Booker T. Washington and his Tuskegee political machine. By the time W.E.B. Du Bois, the man who becomes Washington's rival, rose to international prominence after Washington's death in 1915, Wells-Barnett was marginalized to local Black leadership in her last years. (Ironically, Du Bois' organization, the National Association for the Advancement of Colored People [the NAACP], would assist mightily in making sure that marginalization happened!)

Wells-Barnett attempted to be part of the newly-formed NAACP until she was convinced her leadership and her personality would never really be welcomed there. She helped found the National Association of Colored Women. She had to found the Negro Fellowship League and the National Equal Rights League so that she could direct herself without interference from the more conservative forces in the local and national Black community. But ultimately, she did not have the resources to fight the political maneuvering of the Washington forces. (Washington, for instance, could and did buy Black publications and activists.) But she never surrendered; she might be momentarily disappointed in organizations, but would never give up organizing. Defeat, she believed, was just a prologue to more work.

NAACP

The group of white progressives issued a document named "The Call" in 1909 as a response to the slaughter of Blacks in Springfield, Illinois, somewhat ironically the resting place of President Abraham Lincoln. It was issued because it was time for an organized, activist response to the violent repression of Blacks. The National

Negro Conference was scheduled to take place in New York City. Sixty persons responded to "The Call"; the few Blacks who responded were Atlanta University professor W.E.B. Du Bois, Wells-Barnett, and civil rights activist and suffragist Mary Church Terrell. Wells and Terrell were the only Black women signers.

Wells-Barnett was one of the panelists who spoke at the conference. Her speech was entitled, "Lynching, Our National Crime." She cited 3,824 Black people who had been lynched since Reconstruction.[58] She connected the relationship between the lack of citizenship and lynching.[59] She called for the support of anti-lynching legislation and an investigative bureau that would publish the facts of, and behind, a lynching. She said this would be important because the white press was cheering the white mob.[60]

The tone of the meeting was militant, and Wells-Barnett was determined to keep it that way. She quelled the fears of radicals like William Monroe Trotter that Washington and his political allies were going to be dominant conference players.[61] (They were not.) Trotter and Wells challenged the white liberals who had organized the National Negro Conference to make sure that their concerns were met. In his account of the NAACP's founding, Du Bois referred to Wells-Barnett indirectly, not respecting her enough to name her: "A woman leapt to her feet and cried in passionate, almost tearful earnestness—an earnestness born of bitter experience—'They are betraying us again—these white friends of ours.'"[62]

The meeting went continued. Resolutions were passed. And then Du Bois read the names of the Founding Forty. Washington was not on the list. But neither were the meeting's militant faction, which included Wells-Barnett. She had been told she was on the list, but had been thwarted. One of the conference organizers, Mary White Ovington—who would later become a board member, executive secretary and chair of the NAACP—walked past her "with an air of triumph and a very pleased look on her face."[63]

Du Bois told her that it was he who had removed her, saying he wanted others from the Niagara Movement—the Black-led ad-hoc configuration of civil rights leaders formed in 1905—to represent the group instead. Giddings postulated it was Ovington who was the power behind the throne. The people replacing the militants on the list were people like Ovington.

In her accounts on the founding of the NAACP, Ovington felt that Wells-Barnett was too independent to play the NAACP's relatively genteel game. She and Trotter were "fitted for courageous work, but perhaps not fitted to accept the restraint of organization."[64] She also wrote that Wells "was a great fighter, but we knew that she had to play a lone hand. And if you have too many fighters of lone hands in your organization, you soon have no game."[65]

Du Bois, Giddings hypothesized, might have wanted Wells-Barnett out as well, since he wanted his relationships with white women like Ovington to be free of Wells-Barnett's condescending attitude toward him as her protégé.[66] The white women civil rights activists around Du Bois, Giddings argued, were also becoming experts on Black female migrants, an idea Wells-Barnett did not like because of the assumptions they made about the character of such women.[67]

They added her name to the list at the last minute: Charles Edward Russell "illegally" put her name on the list, wrote Ovington.[68] She was hurt by this experience, and let the NAACP move forward without her.

Later, the NAACP national office would omit Wells-Barnett from the history of the lynching campaign she had led for 20 years before the organization was formed. The official history of lynching crusades, written by NAACP leaders such as Ovington, did not mention her by name. And the NAACP's Chicago chapter, wanting money from the philanthropists that supported Booker T. Washington, would organize around her, not allowing her any real role. As Giddings wrote: "Ida's temperament and the organization's elitism, however, were not the only issues that kept her outside the NAACP leadership. Her ideology and militant views were something that the civil rights organization could, literally, not afford."[69]

NACW

Wells-Barnett was part of the formation of the first national Black women's organization, the National Association of Colored Women. Two Black women's organizations had decided to meet concurrently in 1899, and one of them was the NACW. The other was the Afro-American Council. Giddings quoted Wells-Barnett, who attended the historic joint meeting, in saying she was "the outsider within" each.[70]

How could Ida B. Wells-Barnett be an outsider in an organization of Black women? The answer was the changing wind in national Black leadership. It was blowing cold and conservative. There was a "growing ideological divide" between Wells-Barnett and local clubwomen leadership.[71] The leaders of these movements were moving more and more toward the perspective of Booker T. Washington, one that emphasized industry over civil rights.

Even a Black periodical turned against her in this instance. *The Colored American*, a Black magazine that Washington would buy in 1904, tried to push her out of the Council's financial secretary positon. The magazine claimed her duties as wife and mother would interfere with the work.

Meanwhile, Wells-Barnett found out she was going to be excluded from the NACW program where Washington was going to speak. She didn't even get invited to speak on the NACW's program against lynching. Her militant politics left her politically victimized within the group; the women chosen to lead the organization were Washington devotees.

Wells-Barnett would eventually head the Council's anti-lynching bureau, which gave her power to publish a pamphlet about her activist passion. But eventfully, Washington's forces would take over the Council.

NFL and NERL

During the time of founding of the NAACP, Wells-Barnett was involved in two groups. One of the groups (National Equal Rights League) was political, and the other (the Negro Fellowship League) was social-cultural.

The Negro Fellowship League was Wells-Barnett's attempt to establish her own Black cultural center, a settlement house. In 1909 she had created a place for reading and for listening to lectures. It also included an employment center and a lodging house. Recalled Wells-Barnett: "At the end of our first year we had a registration average of forty to fifty persons a day who came in to read or play checkers or look for jobs."[72] For about a decade, she struggled to keep it financially afloat. Amid funding problems and competition from a local chapter of a new national organization providing similar services, the National Urban League, she closed the NFL's doors in late 1920. Her daughter Alfreda wrote: "She sought the kind of financial help and cooperation from these [middle and upper-class Chicago] Negroes that [activist/social reformer] Jane Addams was able to secure from whites for Hull House. In this she was disappointed."[73]

In 1915, as the NAACP began to consolidate ideologically after Washington's death, Wells-Barnett and the other radical at the 1909 National Negro Conference, William Monroe Trotter, were leaders of an organization they hoped would take more militant stands—the National Equal Rights League. Wells-Barnett was the group's vice-president. The NERL attempted to organize nationally and to get its agenda seen: one of the ideas it proposed was to add to President Woodrow Wilson's fourteen-point program for peace after World War I. The group wanted a fifteenth point: one eliminating any legal and civil distinctions based on race anywhere in the world. She left the group in 1919 because members were upset that Wells-Barnett had presented a resolution in NERL's name—one reacting to a white riot that killed several hundred Blacks in Arkansas, where she called on Blacks to leave the state—at a mass meeting without checking first with the group.

Ida B. Wells-Barnett struggled within organizations because it matched her own internal struggle between independence and conformity, between radical, impulsive acts and well thought-out strategy, between throwing a brick and writing a manifesto. She was both an organization woman and a wild card.

CHAPTER SEVEN
Family Time

As a teenager, Ida B. Wells fought to keep her siblings together after their parents and their infant brother died from the 1878 yellow fever epidemic that tore through Holly Springs, Mississippi. She had made teaching, then journalism, then anti-lynching work her respective vocations. Approaching middle age, her new challenge was to create a family of her own.

Wells was flirty and enjoyed the company of men, but did not suffer fools gladly. She was courted by many suitors, but she was looking for someone who understood her and would take her as an intellectual, spiritual, social and political equal.

She had been familiar with Ferdinand Barnett, a Black Chicago lawyer and anti-lynching activist who edited *The Conservator*, a Black newspaper, for some time. The feminist and believer in armed self-defense was one of the radicals who, like Wells, had accepted Frederick Douglass' position: that he was going to legitimize the 1893 World's Columbian Exposition, a fair celebrating America's (white) achievements since Columbus, by speaking on "Jubilee Day," August 25, a special day the event's organizers set aside for Blacks.[74] Wells, Douglass, Barnett and teacher/writer I. Garland Penn published a pamphlet distributed the day Douglass spoke. It was called *The Reason Why the Colored American Is Not in the World's Columbian Exposition: The Afro-American's Contribution to Columbian Literature*. Today that pamphlet, a manifesto explaining the oppressed condition of Blacks in America, would be called a "State of Black America" or a "Black Agenda" document.[75]

She had worked with Barnett, whom she had met in between her trips to England, and liked him. That affection grew. (She had used *The Conservator*'s offices as the pamphlet's return address.) But she still had her life, which at that point was speaking and getting subscriptions. Unfortunately, he had to accept that all her traveling and speaking did not result in the money white female suffragists had received. She decided that now, her early thirties, was family time.

Wells, ever independent and dutiful, fulfilled her speaking obligations before settling on a wedding date.

She married Ferdinand on June 27, 1895, at Chicago's AME Bethel Church. Wells now was the hyphenated Wells-Barnett, a wife and a stepmother of two sons from Barnett's first marriage, Ferdinand III and Albert. Wells-Barnett and Ferdinand would together produce four more children: Charles (who, as "Baby Barnett," had the honor of having the abolitionist freedom fighter Harriet Tubman hold him up over her head to the delegates who had met to establish the National Association of Colored Women), Herman, Ida Jr. and Alfreda—the daughter who would publish her mother's posthumous, and unfinished, autobiography in 1970.

Wells-Barnett was not deserting the anti-lynching cause. She had decided to have what in the twenty-first century would be considered a typical marriage of balancing motherhood and professional work at *The Conservator*. She purchased the newspaper from its stockholders, which included her husband. For the first time in three years, she had her own newspaper again.

Her domestic situation was in no way typical for the late nineteenth century. It wasn't just that Ferdinand was a feminist who had no problem with either Ida's schedule or doing the cooking.[76] It also wasn't just that she also had domestic help. It was not typical because of who she had been before becoming Mrs. Ida B. Wells-Barnett, her life of service before the hyphen and new title.

She explains in her autobiography the not-so-gentle conflict she had in 1895 with one of her mentors, the suffragist leader Susan B. Anthony, with whom she stayed while attending the memorial of Frederick Douglass:

> I had been with her several days before I noticed the way she would

bite out my married name in addressing me. Finally I said to her, "Miss Anthony, don't you believe in women getting married?" She said, "Oh, yes, but not women like you who had a special call for special work. I too might have married but it would have meant dropping the work to which I had set my hand." She said, "I know of no one in all this country better fitted to do the work you had in hand than yourself. Since you have gotten married, agitation seems practically to have ceased. Besides, you have a divided duty. You are here [in New York] trying to help in the formation of this league [the Afro-American League, a civil rights organization founded and led by Black journalist T. Thomas Fortune; Wells-Barnett was part of a conversation to help re-form it] and your eleven-month-old baby needs your attention at home. You are distracted over the thought that maybe he is not being looked after as he would be if you were there, and that makes for a divided duty."[77]

Wells-Barnett continued to balance work and family. In Chicago, she now had a permanent home—a brownstone on a street in 2017 now called 3624 S. Martin Luther King Drive in Chicago, Illinois. The Barnetts would work and live in that home from 1919 to 1929, in a building that became a National Historic Landmark in 2017. Because of family, not despite it, she kept her equilibrium—her "special call for special work"—for the remainder of her public and private lives. She would keep her hand steady until the last sentence of her autobiography.

CHAPTER EIGHT
Sexism in the Movement: Wells-Barnett Fights Black Female Invisibilty

Ida B. Wells-Barnett was admired by many of her race her entire life. From several quarters, she was venerated by Black activists of both genders as a militant fighter for Black rights. But that did not mean they all wanted to work with her, endorse her or remember her properly when she joined her Ancestors. She had the same traits that, if she had been a man, she would have been praised for: independence, fierceness, bravery, initiative, outspokenness. But as a woman, many Black male leaders—William Monroe Trotter being the great exception—tended to turn away from her in one form or another. Another method of dealing with her was to attempt to turn her anti-lynching campaign work, and, by extension, her life, invisible.

Black men have always praised the ability of Black women to be the shock troops of any movement. But shock troops are always stuck on the ground, doing the grubby work in the dirt; they are not the generals who sit for portraits and write diaries and autobiographies. Wells-Barnett proudly did all three privileged leader-tasks, because she was a proud general. She had trained herself to lead since she took over her family at the age of 16. She could be a follower, but only of people she fully trusted. She could be relatively compliant, but only in the presence of men she fully respected. Sadly, Black men, steeped in the sexism of their time, would not play reciprocal roles, would not fully accept her aggressive leadership style and often-sharp attitude. Wells-Barnett was alternately hurt and angry by this, but she was in a struggle, so she struggled.

Here are two main examples of this Black male-female dynamic happening throughout Wells-Barnett's public career. The first one is an attempt by the abolitionist Frederick Douglass, whom Wells considered a friend and mentor, to subtly diminish her. The second is the total of attempts by national Black male luminaries to turn her work invisible in her later life and minimize it in death.

Example One: The 1894 Frederick Douglass Recommendation Letter And The Non-Rebuke

While in the United Kingdom in 1894, Wells needed a letter from Frederick Douglass to gain the support she needed to be respected at the public halls in which she was attending and speaking. Douglass wrote one of Wells' would-be allies in England, the pacifist pastor Charles Aked, and said of her:

> Miss Ida B. Wells, now sojourning in England, known to me by the persecutions she has been subjected on account of her bold exposures and pungent denunciations of Southern outrages upon Colored

people, has told me of the kindness and help she has received at your hands. Once an exile in your land, I know of the value of such help you have given Miss Wells.[78]

He also enclosed a copy of a speech he had made at the Metropolitan AME Church in Washington, D.C., talking about the white-woman-rape lie that led to lynching. "Although his message echoed that of Wells," Giddings wrote, "Douglass never uttered her name in the speech."[79]

The letter and the speech were less than a ringing endorsement; Giddings called the effort's total "short of accrediting Ida."[80] Douglass acted as if he didn't even know Wells very well. This letter was written after Wells, a loyal foot-soldier to the older man, had sat in his home and even helped Douglass write the Columbian Exposition pamphlet. Where was the man who wrote the glowing 1892 testimonial in *The New York Age*, which Wells reprinted as a preface to *Southern Horrors*? Was this an example of an old man being jealous of a younger activist going to England and being praised for her bravery and articulate passion, the way he did and had been decades ago? And/or was this a recognized leader who was openly reluctant to give Wells, an equally brave and committed Black woman, the same status he, a Black man, enjoyed with the British? Giddings categorized the tone of this letter by Douglass to Aked as "the strategy of faint praise to restore order to the world."[81] In subsequent letters and a cable-gram about Wells, he still refused to endorse her completely.[82]

What was even more distressing, per Giddings, is that Douglass—trying to remain "relevant in the political scheme of things" in Washington, D.C.—publicly praised C.H.J. Taylor, a Black newspaper editor who had publicly attacked Wells. Douglass was helping Taylor so that he could keep a prestigious job, the government job of recorder of deeds; it was the same post that the great abolitionist once held.[83] Douglass ignored Taylor's written savagery against Wells, which included a public call to "muzzle" that "animal from Memphis."[84]

Example Two: Pioneering National Anti-Lynching Campaign? *What* Pioneering National Anti-Lynching Campaign?

Somehow, Black leaders and luminaries had forgotten that Ida B. Wells, as a young woman, was a pioneering anti-lynching activist, launching campaigns around the nation and speaking out in Europe against the topic. They had also seemingly forgotten that she was still doing that type of work almost up until the time of her illness. Giddings wrote:

> When, in 1930, *The Chicago Defender* announced a list of fifty prominent leaders, put together by the muckraking journalist Ida Tarbell, whose exposés succeeding those of Wells-Barnett, Mary

McLeod Bethune was mentioned, but not Ida. Her name was also missing from *Who's Who in Colored America*, a 499-page biographical dictionary, which covered the years 1930 to 1932. [NAACP leader] Walter White's 1928 publication, *Rope and Faggot*, which became a classic text on lynching, also left Ida's name out.

The most disturbing evidence that the substance of her accomplishment was forgotten was when she and her daughter Ida [Jr.] attended a local Negro history club meeting to discuss a book written by Black historian Carter G. Woodson, the "father of Negro history." As she ruefully noted in her daybook, there was "no mention of my anti-lynching contribution." Ironically, Ida had hosted Woodson at the Negro Fellowship League at the very time he was launching the Association of Negro Life and History.[85]

Giddings also pointed out that when Wells-Barnett died, *Crisis* editor W.E.B. Du Bois, who, as previously mentioned, did not exactly champion her for leadership in the NAACP, wrote—in a way that the Wells biographer correctly describes as "churlish"—that although Wells-Barnett was a pioneering anti-lynching crusader, her work had been overlooked because of the much larger, more successful work of the NAACP.[86]

Ida B. Wells-Barnett was a Black woman working for the protection and eventual liberation of Black communities. That meant that she was used to invisible rewards. But there is a difference between invisible rewards and *contemporary, and ultimately historic, invisibility*. This is especially true when that public condition is created and maintained by Black men for no other reason than to satisfy the Black male ego. It was disheartening to Wells-Barnett to find that attitude among brave "race men"—tested freedom fighters—who were willing to risk their lives for the cause of African-Americans. But there it was.

This chapter is not just about Ida B. Wells-Barnett. It's also the (post-) modern story of any Black woman who decides to become a Black community activist. Because Black women activists were—and still are—determined to save the *entire* Black race, not only from white people, but also from itself. That commitment always creates unnecessary and ever-troublesome burdens for them, ones they must acknowledge, grapple with, publicly denounce, absorb, and then ultimately move on from before they destroy the spirit-force needed to rescue and reconstruct a people.

CHAPTER NINE
The Complicated Relationship Between Wells-Barnett and White Feminism

In her long life, Ida B. Wells-Barnett had to balance many competing interests: teaching and writing, launching into anti-lynching campaigns and creating a stable family life, and, perhaps most important, her work as a Black feminist.

That last listed role—by definition an amalgam of competing interests, since it is a never-ending balancing act between the needs of the Black community vs. the social and political struggles of her fellow women whose skin is white—have filled shelves of books throughout the twentieth and twenty-first centuries. But Wells didn't have access to those books during her life, because they hadn't been written yet. She couldn't ask for advice from the most prominent twentieth century Black feminists, because most of them hadn't been born yet. With few exceptions—Mary Church Terrell and Harriet Tubman being the obvious choices, since Sojourner Truth died when Wells was only 21 and not yet established on her life's journey—she couldn't ask for advice from her fellow nineteenth century Black feminists, because she was too busy being one. In Black journalism, she had the models of Mary Ann Shadd Cary, T. Thomas Fortune, Frederick Douglass and many others, including the founders of the Black press, John Brown Russwurm and Samuel Cornish, in which to draw collective strength. But in helping to create Black feminism—which required an often-complicated relationship with white feminism, especially the predominately white suffragist movement—she and her fellow Black clubwomen were on their own, with roads to create.

Rosalyn Terborg-Penn, the historian from Morgan State University, wrote:

Black women, in their struggle for the right to vote, fought racism and sexism simultaneously and revealed several things about the nature of their struggle as women suffragists. First, although Black men appeared to be in the forefront throughout the duration of the movement, they occupied positions of prominence primarily during the first forty years. From the last decade of the nineteenth century to the end of the struggle for the Nineteenth Amendment, more Black women than men took leadership positions. Leadership was manifested in local and regional woman suffrage activities, although coalitions of African American women and men organized in the struggle for women's right to vote.

In addition, African American women developed multiple levels of consciousness in their political struggle, as Black women's support for woman suffrage often paralleled, *yet developed differently from that of white suffragists, especially as the movement progressed.* Although strategies were similar and there were coalitions between Blacks and whites, the experiences of the two racial groups differed. The existence of racism resulting in an anti-Black woman suffrage agenda and tactics among many whites, and the racial discrimination among African American women encountered at the polls, reinforced differences among Black and white women suffragists.[87]

There were three instances that Ida B. Wells-Barnett recalled during her life that, sadly, demonstrate this "different development" along racial lines. They were 1) a discussion between suffragist leader Susan B. Anthony and Wells-Barnett about Frederick Douglass; 2) Wells-Barnett's response to an article that suffragist leader Jane Addams wrote, and 3) Wells-Barnett's participation in a predominately white suffragist parade in Washington, D.C. in 1913.

In each case, Wells-Barnett had to stand up for herself as a Black woman while simultaneously showing solidarity with her white comrades.

Wells and Anthony On Frederick Douglass vs. The National American Women's Suffrage Association (NAWSA)

In the spring of 1895, Susan B. Anthony, the leader of the predominantly white suffragist movement, entertained Wells at her home in Rochester, New York. It was the first of several conversations the two would have at Anthony's house over the years.

This first one, however, distressed the younger Black woman. They talked about the great abolitionist leader Frederick Douglass, also a powerful voice in the suffragist movement.

There had been a significant change in that movement within the last five years.

It was consolidating nationally. The NAWSA, the National American Women's Suffrage Association, was formed in 1890 as the merger of two organizations, the American Women Suffrage Association and the National Women's Suffrage Association. The new organization, now led by Anthony, wanted to attract white Southern women and had begun to distance itself from Blacks and their causes.[88]

Anthony—"perhaps guiltily," wrote Giddings—told Wells that she had convinced Douglass not to attend that January's NAWSA meeting in Atlanta.[89] It was the first time the group had met in the South, and Anthony did not want any racial disruptions—especially the alienation of the white Southen women—it might cause.[90] "Moreover, while in Atlanta," continued Giddings, "Anthony had refused the request from a group of Black women to help them establish a Black branch of the suffrage organization."[91]

Wells-Barnett wrote about the exchange in her Autobiography. "'...And do you think I was wrong is so doing?' she [Anthony] asked. I answered uncompromisingly yes, for I felt that although she may have gain[ed] for suffrage, she had also confirmed white women in their attitude of segregation."[92] Wells-Barnett then praises Anthony, whom she clearly saw as a pioneer and a kind of mentor, for her intellectual fairness and her leadership.[93]

Jane Addams 1901 *Independent* Article and Wells-Barnett's Response

In 1901, Jane Addams, the social reformer and suffragist, wrote an anti-lynching article in *The Independent*, an important white periodical of the time. It was so unintentionally outrageous that Wells-Barnett had to respond to it.

In the article, called "Respect For Law," Addams attempted to straddle the fence on the issue, saying that if working-class Blacks committed crimes worthy of lynching (she didn't mention the rape of white women specifically), that the punishment would do no good:

> Brutality begets brutality; and proceeding on the theory that the negro is undeveloped, and therefore must be treated in this primitive fashion, is to forget that the immature pay little attention to statements, but quickly imitate what they see. The under-developed are never helped by such methods as these, for they learn only by imitation. The child who is managed by a system of bullying and terrorizing is almost sure to be the vicious and stupid child.[94]

So was lynching just a problem of the wrong remedy for the crimes committed by "undeveloped" or "under-developed" working-class Blacks? This seemed to be what Addams was saying about what in the twenty-first century would be considered blatant human rights violations in defiance of the U.S. Constitution.

Wells-Barnett wrote a response, also printed in *The Independent*, that was gentle to the prominent white female leader, but also clear about the problem. In the beginning, she thanks Addams, but then adds:

> At the same time an unfortunate presumption used as a basis for her argument works so serious, tho doubtless unintentional, an injury to the memory of thousands of victims of mob law, that it is only fair to call attention to this phase of the writer's plea. It is unspeakably infamous to put thousands of people to death without a trial by jury; it adds to that infamy to charge that these victims were moral monsters, when, in fact, four-fifths of them were not so accused even by the fiends who murdered them.[95]

She continued that Addams' assumption that the lynched may be guilty because of some supposed class difference was extremely flawed:

> It is this assumption, this absolutely unwarrantable assumption, that

vitiates every suggestion which it inspires Miss Addams to make. It is the same baseless assumption which influences ninety-nine out of every one hundred persons who discuss this question. Among many thousand editorial clippings I have received in the past five years, ninety-nine per cent, discuss the question upon the presumption that lynchings are the desperate effort of the Southern people to protect their women from black monsters, and while the large majority condemn lynching, the condemnation is tempered with a plea for the lyncher — that human nature gives way under such awful provocation and that the mob, insane for the moment, must be pitied as well as condemned. It is strange that an intelligent, law-abiding and fair minded people should so persistently shut their eyes to the facts in the discussion of what the civilized world now concedes to be America's national crime.

This almost universal tendency to accept as true the slander which the lynchers offer to civilization as an excuse for their crime might be explained if the true facts were difficult to obtain. But not the slightest difficulty intervenes. The Associated Press dispatches, the press clipping bureau, frequent book publications and the annual summary of a number of influential journals give the lynching record every year. This record, easily within the reach of every one who wants it, makes inexcusable the statement and cruelly unwarranted the assumption that negroes are lynched only because of their assaults upon womanhood.[96]

She then showed the record, and discussed how many lynched were middle-class. Showing that even Black women get lynched—five were in the last five years, she pointed out—she warned against making any presumptions about who gets lynched.

The fact that she had to take this much space and time, not to intellectually engage an enemy, but to correct an *ally*, shows how difficult it was for Black Americans to work with whites who not only had access to significant public resources, but also, sadly, to the inbred poison of white supremacy and class elitism. What in the twenty-first century is called white privilege proliferated in movements led by well-meaning whites. Addams, for example, could afford to be ignorant and not look up facts and statistics when discussing other groups; Wells-Barnett, part of two oppressed groups (Blacks and the poor), did not have those privileges.

The Jim-Crowed NAWSA Suffrage March

The NAWSA decided to have a suffrage parade in Washington, D.C. in 1913. Unfortunately, this march for the civil rights of women wanted to keep the delegation all-white, shocking the Black would-be participants, including Wells-Barnett. The NAWSA did not want any racial issues, whether in a Jim-Crowed Congress or a genteel Jim Crowed-NAWSA, to damage a possible suffrage amendment.

Wells-Barnett, who had arrived in town with the 62-member Illinois delegation, was understandably enraged. She wanted the delegation from her own state, Illinois, to fight the NAWSA national leadership. "If the Illinois women do not take a stand now in this great democratic parade then colored women are lost," she said through her tears. Ultimately, she was told not to march with the now all-white Illinois delegation, but in the back with the Black delegation. She defied the edict, and marched down Pennsylvania Avenue with Illinois delegation members Virginia Brooks and Belle Squire: "Each had a satisfied look on her face," wrote Giddings, describing *The Chicago Tribune* photo of the trio.[97]

Terborg-Penn discusses this incident in her book, and adds this important point:

> To put this discussion in context, it does not matter if contemporary historians debate whether or not white suffragists were racists. The point here is that Black leaders of the time believed that white suffragists were racists. African Americans did not trust the actions of the white suffragists, which Black leaders believed were exclusionary on the basis of their race.[98]

As usual, Wells-Barnett would define her own role; she would think, act and speak as she saw fit. She would neither ignore racism within the suffragist ranks nor castigate her white female allies as racists. She knew that there were many struggles that Black women were part of, acknowledged or not, voluntary or not. And all she had ever known was that she had to stand up for herself—to shake the rafters, whether she was standing on them or not.

CHAPTER TEN
An Elder in the 20th Century Black Freedom Movement

In the twentieth century, Ida B. Wells-Barnett, now a full member of Black Chicago's top leadership, was an elder stateswoman in the struggle for Black emancipation. Her bravery and work had made her a local, national and international name among those who struggled for Black equality and self-determination. At the turn of the century, she had already seen herself as a kind of mentor to W.E.B. Du Bois, who had become a powerful leader of the NAACP, and as an admirer and junior stateswoman of sorts to abolitionist statesman Frederick Douglass. She considered the activist-journalist William Monroe Trotter a peer. Now, in her last 30 years, she interacted with many of the younger activists who would have a major impact in the new century since the death of Booker T. Washington in 1915. The new-century leaders she met included mass movement leader Marcus Garvey and labor union organizer Asa Philip Randolph. Like Wells-Barnett before them, both Garvey and Randolph (and W.E.B. Du Bois as well) used journalism as a vehicle for activism. Leaders such as Randolph and Garvey would become the kind of leaders of direct-action mass movements that Wells-Barnett, if not for the blatant sexism of the time, could have led.

The challenge for Wells-Barnett was no longer attempting to fit into an organization, for she had founded and/or worked with many; it was now deciding what kind of public leadership role she should hold in Chicago. She would try her hand at being a political kingmaker, a delegate and a political candidate. She would never be afraid to try or fail at something that resembled progress for Black people, particularly newly-enfranchised Black women in Chicago.

Wells-Barnett would continue her anti-lynching and suffragist crusades into the first three decades of the twentieth century. The new century would bring new challenges. Changes in immigration, industrialization and transportation would create new concentrations of people. Jim Crow's institutionalization would create stronger Black communities that would, in turn, demand (and be able to sustain) stronger Black media (and Black activism) vehicles. The twentieth century, the time of mass society and the Age of Mass Media, was underway in her last years, and Wells' example of Black press journalistic advocacy was well established by the time of her death in 1931.

In June of 1917, some interesting partnerships between Black leaders were being made. Trotter and Wells' National Equal Rights League had found a like-minded organization—the Liberty League. The New York-based group was headed by Hubert Henry Harrison, a man who, like Wells, was very militant and could rub people the wrong way. Harrison was one of the greatest Black thinkers of the early twentieth century. The Liberty League featured that month a young man who had emigrated from Jamaica—Marcus Garvey. The Jamaican activist would soon be the leader of the largest mass movement of Black Americans in the history of Black America.

Wells-Barnett, per Giddings, had "probably" met Garvey in 1917, when he was shuttling around the nation, meeting Black leaders like Ferdinand Barnett.[99] Garvey, who had formed the United Negro Improvement Association by then, had been invited by the Barnetts to dinner, where the younger man explained the origins of his program—that he had been angered by the exploitation of Blacks he had seen in America and in the Caribbean, and that he had been inspired by the institution-building example of Booker T. Washington. The following year—in 1918, the same year the UNIA's newspaper, *The Negro World* was founded— Garvey invited Wells-Barnett to speak at a Harlem meeting of the UNIA.

At the meeting, there was another man who was on the speaking slate who, like Garvey, would shape the first half of the twentieth century—A. Philip Randolph. He had already been arrested for sedition for publishing in his *Messenger* magazine, a Black radical publication, that Blacks should physically fight for freedom in America, not in France.

By speaking at that rally, Wells-Barnett had set herself firmly in the historic continuum of Black activism. Actually, this modern continuum—of activism and radical Black journalism—was *hers* to share with the younger men, both of whom had national publications at the time.

She got placed in another, evil continuum as well; the federal government had begun to spy on her. Wrote Giddings: "Indeed, both Garvey and Wells-Barnett were seen as potential threats in this regard, but Ida, with her longer track record, was deemed especially worrisome."[100] As a result, the federal government stopped the plans of Wells-Barnett, Trotter and Madam C.J. Walker, a Black businesswoman who was involved in Black affairs, to be delegates at the 1919 Paris Peace Conference by denying their passports.[101] The trio was going to talk about the oppression that Blacks faced in America, and Wells-Barnett was going as a UNIA representative.

In 1926, Wells-Barnett attended a mass meeting of the newly-formed Brotherhood of Sleeping Car Porters. A. Philip Randolph had been recruited by union members, inspired by his *Messenger* editorials, to head it. She endorsed Randolph's leadership against the white Pullman Company as he fought to establish a Chicago chapter of the all-Black union. She defended him against the public opposition that came from the editorial pages of *The Chicago Defender*, then becoming a "national" Black newspaper powerhouse.

Wells-Barnett understood before it became a cliché that all politics is local. So after fighting for the right of women to vote, she decided to fight for them to utilize that vote locally. She founded the Third Ward

Women's Political Club in 1927. Wells-Barnett had always been active in Chicago politics through her Black women's clubs, and now she hoped her decades of groundwork would pay off. The new club would not only mobilize the get-out-the-vote effort for Black candidates, but would also organize women to run for public office.

In 1928, an election year, Wells-Barnett practiced what she preached: she ran for a Republican National Convention delegate seat, from the First Congressional District. Unfortunately, she was crushed by Oscar DePriest and Daniel Jackson, well-entrenched Black candidates who had the support of *The Chicago Defender* and certain segments of the Black community.[102]

She also decided to run for office herself, becoming a candidate for a State Senate seat in 1930. She lost.

To the day she fell ill, she continued to fight against the abuses suffered by African-Americans.

She also began writing her autobiography to make sure her contributions would be known. The book ends in mid-sentence, with her fighting the racial segregation of a Chicago hotel: "I also received some beautiful letters from members of the board of directors thanking us for calling attention to what was go-"[103]

—§—

Ida B. Wells-Barnett died in Chicago on March 15, 1931, from kidney poisoning. She was 68. The Metropolitan Church was packed in what was called by newspaper accounts an unpretentious funeral. Sons Herman and Charles, stepsons Albert and Ferdinand Jr., and nephews Emory and Jack Wells, respectively, the sons of her brothers Alfred James and George, were the pallbearers.

Her fight to define and preserve her role in Black public memory would have a long hiatus. Her unfinished autobiography, edited by her daughter Alfreda M. Duster, would be first published in 1970. Her diary, documenting her days as a young woman in Memphis, would be published twenty-five years later. Her articles would remain uncollected for the remainder of the century, but her lynching pamphlets would be made available on the World Wide Web and in at least one book collection.[104]

With Black history in Black-Power vogue and the publication of her autobiography during that specific time, Ida B. Wells-Barnett was rediscovered by a generation of Blacks and women—particularly those interested in journalism—who grew up with both the Black Power and feminist movements. By 2017, at least four major biographies of her life would be published, and a substantial collection of her writings would be assembled.[105] And she would also become by then a perennial favorite of children's book authors, joining such nineteenth century Black woman icons as Sojourner Truth and Harriet Tubman.

But that was just the beginning of her life's impact. As nineteenth and early twentieth century journalism became twentieth and twenty-first century mass (and now, *de-massified*) media, and the Black direct-action mass activism she saw in Garvey's and Randolph's respective movements became the twentieth and twenty-first century norm, it turned out that Wells-Barnett had many, many spiritual children, grandchildren, and great-grandchildren—in journalism, activism, and in any shade of combination between the two vocations.

CODA
A Nation of Leading Black Female Voices

Ida B. Wells-Barnett is the bridge between America's post-Civil War period and mid-twentieth century America. But she is also the inspiration for both Black female journalists of all types as well as those Black female activists who, using social media, agitate and organize around state-sanctioned violence against African-Americans.

She paved the way for many pioneering Black female journalists in the Black press between the period between World War II the Civil Rights Movement and beyond, including: Ethel Payne of *The Chicago Defender*; Evelyn Cunningham of *The Pittsburgh Courier*; Alice Dunnigan and Eslanda Robeson (the activist wife of Paul Robeson) of the Associated Negro Press wire service, and Utrice Leid of The Trans-Urban News Service, a New York-based wire service that became a short-lived, muckraking, often-militant mid-1980s-to-1990s tabloid newspaper, *The* (Brooklyn, N.Y.) *City Sun*. In 2017, it is in no way unusual that Black newspapers across the nation have female editors and publishers. Hazel Trice Edney—a former editor of the NNPA (National Newspaper Publishers Association) News Service, the nation's sole surviving national Black-oriented wire service for Black newspapers from the 1970s into the twenty-first century—started her own wire service, the Trice Edney News Wire, in 2010. In 2017, the NNPA News Service became one of her clients. Edney and the Black female staff reporters, editors and publishers working for Black newspapers all claim Wells-Barnett as a patron saint of their collective vocation.

Black women continued to ascend in American mass media after the start of desegregation in American newsrooms in the 1960s. Top Black reporters—like PBS's Charlyane Hunter-Gault, the late Gwen Ifill of PBS and Isabel Wilkerson, a former *New York Times* reporter who wrote a major nonfiction book on the major migration of Blacks to Northern cities during the twentieth century— became pioneers of race and gender desegregation in American mainstream news media, and, thus, role models for twenty-first century Black women who wanted careers in such media.

Because of the development of mainstream Black journalism, Ida B. Wells-Barnett became a name heralded and appropriated by these Black mainstream journalists. In 1975, the National Association of Black Journalists, a professional organization created to increase Black participation in the mainstream media, was founded. It and Northwestern University's Medill School of Journalism annually give out an award in Wells-Barnett's name to a person or corporation that increased opportunities for journalists of color in the mainstream media. And in 2016, a small group of Black mainstream top investigative journalists met in Memphis to form the Ida B. Wells Society for Investigative Reporting. The group's mission is to train young investigative journalists of color.

The society is headquartered and sponsored by the City University of New York's Graduate School of Journalism in New York City.

Concurrently, Black women became local and national radio and television newscasters starting in the 1970s. Some had a Black activist bent. Susan Taylor hosted a television version of her *Essence* magazine in the 1980s, while Black Entertainment Television hired radio broadcaster Bev Smith to host a weeknight show, "Our Voices," as the decade closed. In the 1990s, April Ryan, a newscaster based in Baltimore, became the White House correspondent for American Urban Radio Networks, a Black radio syndicator. She is still at the White House for the network in 2017, and was named that year as a contributor to CNN.

Meanwhile, in Washington, D.C. a 1980s Black activist call-in radio broadcaster became the nation's largest Black-oriented media owner in the twenty-first century. Cathy Hughes owns and operates TV One, a national cable television entertainment network serving Black audiences. (In 2017, the network ended its airing of "News One Now," a two-hour, weekday morning news discussion program for Black audiences. It was hosted by Black journalist Roland Martin.) She also owns more than 50 radio stations nationwide, and has a radio syndication arm that distributes programs like a weekday call-in talk show by civil rights activist the Rev. Al Sharpton. The School of Communications at historically Black Howard University, a place that has trained many Black journalists, was named after Hughes in 2016.

But there were others that are fellow travelers of Wells-Barnett that don't easily fit the twentieth century paradigm of Black press and/or mainstream press. They are separate but overlapping.

One example was the development of hiphop journalism. In the 1990s, such journalism expanded, creating national platforms for Black women to write about pop culture and Black culture from feminist viewpoints. Those writers include: dream hampton, Joan Morgan, Ericka Blount Danois and Akiba Solomon, among many others. In the twenty-first century, online Black feminist culture writers like Jamilah Lemieux and Rachel Kaadzi Ghansah created significant national online followings. April R. Silver, a former Howard University activist, is a Black feminist writer who became an entrepreneur: Her Akila Worksongs public relations firm links together Black activists of all types.

Black Lives Matter is another example. Founded by activists on Black Twitter who became nationally known on-the-ground workers—Alicia Garza, Patrisse Cullors, Opal Tometi—are Black women. They rang the alarm about nationally publicized, and often videotaped, episodes of police officers fatally shooting Black men—separate-but-frequent incidents which, to many African-American eyes, echoed lynchings.

A third example would be America's Black female "public intellectuals"—advanced-degreed scholars who write and broadcast, or appear on broadcasts, for mainstream audiences. Scholars such as radical activist Rosa Clemente, political scientist Melissa Harris-Perry (who hosted her own advocacy-journalism program on MSNBC during much of Barack Obama's presidency) and law professor Michelle Alexander have advocated for radical reform in America's criminal justice system, as well as other issues concerning Black communities. These women scholars see their public role as advocates for racial and social justice.

Even Wells-Barnett's definitive biographer, Paula Giddings, fits many of the clothes that her subject first wore. In the 1970s, she worked as the Paris Bureau Chief of the *Encore American and Worldwide News* magazine, a national Black magazine. While there, she traveled to South Africa, covering the anti-apartheid movement. In the 1980s, she became a historian who wrote an acclaimed history of Black women in America and a book about the Black sorority Delta Sigma Theta.

(By the time Giddings wrote her book, Black sororities had become major players in African-American social life, expanding the mission of the older Colored women's clubs. And those clubs still exist, on some level: two of the most prominent are the National Congress of Black Women and the National Association of Colored Women's Clubs, the latter co-founded by Wells.)

With more racial incidents, and more opportunities for members of Black grass-roots communities to report on them and to rally against them, there will be more twenty-first century Black (female) activism in the spirit of Ida B. Wells-Barnett.

NOTES

1. Alfeda M. Duster (ed.) *Crusade For Justice: The Autobiography of Ida B. Wells* (Chicago and London: University of Chicago Press, 1970), pp. 7-8. Duster, one of the daughters of Ida B. Wells-Barnett and the editor of her mother's autobiography, described her grandparents in the book's introduction: "Her [Ida's] mother was a deeply religious woman whose convictions about the essential dignity of man developed under the cruelties of slavery. Her father, a man of independent spirit even in slavery, sought and attained his full independence in the period following emancipation. These qualities of her parents fused to add fire and zeal to the character of Ida Wells" (p. xiv).

   Wells writes the following about her father James (pp. 8-9): "After the war was over Mr. Bolling urged his able young apprentice to stay with him. He did until election time. Mr. Bolling wanted him to vote the Democratic ticket, which he refused to do. When he returned from voting he found the shop locked. Jim Wells said nothing to no one, but went downtown, bought a new set of tools, and went across the street and rented another house. When Mr. Bolling returned he found he had lost a workman and a tenant, for already Wells had moved his family off the Bolling place."

Wells recalls a slavery-era conversation between her parents about a "Miss Polly," Morgan Wells' wife, who "had [Wells' grandmother Peggy] stripped and whipped" (p. 10).

2. Duster, p. xv.

3. Paula Giddings, *A Sword Among Lions: Ida B. Wells and the Campaign Against Lynching* (New York: Amistad, 2008). On Page 36, she lists that "[m]ore than four hundred Holly Springs residents died in the epidemic. Among whites, 200

men, 70 women, and 15 children perished. Among Blacks, 70 men, 48 women, and 12 children died. The mortality rates of the 1,440 who were struck by the disease was 71.66 percent among whites and 7.41 percent among Blacks. Per the published death announcements, the Wellses appeared to be the only Black family to suffer multiple mortalities." Giddings' work is considered the definitive biography of Wells-Barnett.

4. Duster, p. 16.

5. *Ibid.*

6. Giddings, p. 13.

7. Wells was not the only Black participant in a train seating scuffle with a white train conductor and a subsequent lawsuit. Ironically, Harriet Tubman—the enslaved African who became first a "conductor" of the Underground Railroad, and later a spy-hero of the Civil War, was almost thrown off a train in October 1865 because of racial discrim-

ination. The incident happened as Tubman was traveling from Philadelphia to New York. Her ticket and government employee explanation was not enough to get acceptance in the obviously white, "half-fare" seat. Like Wells-Barnett, she refused to go to the smoking car, as she had been ordered. "Come, hustle out of here! We don't carry niggers for half-fare," the white conductor barked. They wrestled, and, as Tubman recalls to her as-told-to biographer, Sarah Bradford, four conductors broke her arm while throwing her into the baggage car. No bystander helped her, she claimed, as she writhed in pain all the way to The Empire State. An attempt to sue the railroad company failed for some reason, partly because a witness failed to appear in court. For more on Harriet Tubman, read Bradford's *Scenes in the Life of Harriet Tubman* (Auburn, N.Y.: W. J. Moses, 1869), and Kate Clifford Larson's comprehensive scholarly biography, *Bound for the Promised Land: Harriet Tubman: Portrait of an American Hero*

(New York: One World, 2004). For general audiences, Annette Alston's *Harriet Tubman For Beginners* (Danbury, Connecticut: For Beginners Press, 2017), provides an excellent summary narrative.

8. Miriam DeCosta-Willis (ed), *The Memphis Diary of Ida B. Wells: An Intimate Portrait of the Activist as a Young Woman* (Boston: Beacon Press, 1995), p. 141.

9. Duster, p. 23.

10. *Ibid.*

11. Giddings (p. 78) wrote about Wells' journalistic pseudonym: "There is no explanation for the selection of her pen name, but it is interesting to note that her handwritten name, as it was listed in the 1880 census for Holly Springs, looked like 'Iola.' Since names were often written as census takers heard them, and Ida was probably away when the census taker came to the Wells house, it is possible that 'Iola' was how her name

was pronounced by her younger siblings."

12. Duster, p. 31.

13. *Ibid.*, pp. 35-37.

14. *Ibid.* Wells had asked one of the paper's co-owners, Rev. F. Nightingale, to sign an article for her describing the "utterly inadequate buildings" and "poor teachers" who had "illicit friendship[s] with members of the school board" in Black Memphis schools. He refused, so she ran it. "The worst part of the experience," Wells-Barnett recalled years later, "was the lack of appreciation shown by the parents. They simply couldn't understand why one would risk a good job, even for their children. The burden of their simple refrain was, 'Miss Ida, you ought not to have done it; you might have known that they would fire you.' But I thought it was right to strike a blow against a glaring evil and I did not regret it. Up to that time I had felt that any fight made in the interest of the race

would have its support. I learned that I could not count on that."

15. Lerone Bennett Jr., *The Shaping of Black America* (New York: Penguin Books, 1993 reprint of 1991 revised ed.), 114, 116. Note: Portions of this chapter have appeared in the academic journal article, "'No Other But A Negro Can Represent A Negro': How Black Newspapers 'Founded' Black America and Black Britain," co-written by this author and Olive Vassell, in *The Journal of Pan-African Studies*, 7:4, October 2014, pp. 256-267.

16. *Ibid.,* 121.

17. *Ibid.*

18. Jane Rhodes, *Mary Ann Shadd Cary: The Black Press and Protest in the Nineteenth Century* (Bloomington, Ind.: Indiana University Press, 1998), p. 221. Shadd Cary had several public battles with Black male leaders, especially Henry Bibb, publisher of *The Voice of the Fugitive*, a rival pro-emigration Black

newspaper, before she started *The Freeman*.

19. Shadd, "Adieu," *The Provincial Freeman*, June 30, 1855, p. 2, as quoted in Rodger Streitmatter's *Raising Her Voice: African-American Women Journalists Who Changed History* (Lexington: University of Kentucky) 1994, p. 32.

20. Todd Steven Burroughs, "Drums In The Global Village: Toward an Ideological History of Black Media," Unpublished dissertation (College Park: University of Maryland at College Park, 2001), pp. 66-67. My dissertation attempts to define Black media ideology from a Black nationalist/Afrocentric/African-centered viewpoint.

21. *Ibid.*, p. 71.

22. Bennett, 128.

23. Burroughs, p. 73.

24. "Iola's Southern Field," *New York Age*, November 19, 1892, as printed in Mia Bay's (ed.), *Ida B. Wells: The Light of*

Truth: Writings of an Anti-Lynching Crusader (New York: Penguin Books, 2014), p. 84.

25. Linda O. McMurray, *To Keep The Waters Troubled: The Life of Ida B. Wells* (New York: Oxford University Press, 1998), p. 86.

26. *Ibid.*

27. Duster, p. 40.

28. *Ibid.*

29. Giddings, 2008, p. 183.

30. Duster, p. 55.

31. Undated editorial from Duster, p. 52.

32. Writes Giddings in *Where and When I Enter: The Impact of Black Women on Race and Sex in America* (New York: William Morrow and Co., 1984), p. 29: "Touted as the 'first inside story of Negro lynching,' it included names, dates, places and circumstances of hundreds of lynchings for alleged rape. The response to the article was sensational and For-

tune published ten thousand copies of the issue; one thousand were sold in the streets of Memphis alone." This would be known in pamphlet form as *Southern Horrors: Lynch Law in all its Phases*. Wells' anti-lynching work, including excerpts of the many pamphlets she wrote over the decades, is discussed in detail in Chapter 4.

33. Ta-Nehisi Coates mediates on this concept in the twenty-first century in his book *Between the World and Me* (New York: Spiegel & Grau, 2015).

34. Ida B. Wells (1892), *Southern Horrors: Lynch Law in all its Phases*, as quoted in Mia Bay's (ed.) *The Light of Truth: Writings of an Anti-Lynching Crusader* (New York: Penguin Books, 2014), p. 80.

35. Giddings, p. 313.

36. Giddings, p. 223. Giddings pointed out on page 225 that Wells was careful in the pamphlet to "not claim that no Black man was guilty of rape[.]" She also wrote on page 226 about the South's cultural

growing pains beyond Victorian beliefs: "The sense of chivalry behind the rationales for lynching, Wells was claiming, might have been sincere, but it was inauthentic in a modern age."

37. Ida B. Wells, "Chapter IV: Lynch Law," in Wells, Frederick Douglass and I. Garland Penn (1893). *The Reason The Colored American Is Not in the World's Columbian Exposition: The Afro-American's Contribution to Columbian Literature*, as quoted by Bay, p. 133. Giddings (p. 279) points out that the essay was "written more than a decade before the first scholarly treatment of lynching[.]"

38. *Chicago Daily Inter-Ocean*, July 19, 1893, As quoted in Giddings, p. 275.

39. Giddings, p. 325. Giddings also pointed out that Gov. Turney was the same man who, as a former Tennessee Supreme Court chief, was on the bench when Wells lost her Chesapeake & Ohio railway appeal.

40. Ida B. Wells (1895). *A Red Record*, as published by Bay, p. 224. Giddings (p. 347) wrote: "The new pamphlet showed that ida had not backed down on her critiques, but had refined them. Wells, an increasingly astute student of the social sciences, challenged the pseudoscience of Black regression and acknowledged the role of ideology and psychology in the rape charge. 'The question must be asked,' Wells wrote, 'what the white man means when he charges the Black man with rape. Does he mean the crime which the statutes of the civilized states describe as such? Not by any means,' she continued. Because Southern white men found it 'impossible' to conceive of a voluntary relationship between Black men and white women, Ida explained, they always assumed such liaisons were ones of force."

41. As quoted by Giddings, p. 403.

42. Giddings, pp. 408-409.

43. Ida Wells-Barnett (1899). *Lynch Law in Georgia*, as quoted in Bay, p. 314.

44. *Ibid.*, p. 332.
45. *Ibid.*, pp. 342-343.
46. Giddings, pp. 494-496. The biographer noted (p. 500) that the NAACP had now begun to focus on lynching, and began to imitate Wells-Barnett's approach. They took Wells-Barnett's tactic of hiring detective agencies to get research on a case. It was now focusing "on an issue that was at once important, legitimatized its predominately white existence in the eyes of Blacks, and, largely because of the awareness engendered by Ida's campaign, was capable of attracting funds from not only Blacks but whites. Within a year, the NAACP had sponsored an anti-lynching rally at the Ethnical Culture in New York City, published a sixteen-page pamphlet, *Notes on Lynchings in the United States*, and established an anti-lynching fund that had raised four hundred dollars." Later (p. 558), Giddings wrote this about the NAACP: "Its focus on three areas of activity—information gathering, investi-

gation, and influencing southern business and political leaders to speak out against lynching—borrowed from Wells-Barnett, but did not include the kind of direct action that was the key to her strategies."

She also notes (p. 501) that this was the beginning of the period that the NAACP began to write Wells-Barnett out of the history of national lynching campaigns. "In [NAACP founder Mary White] Ovington's subsequent documentation about the NAACP's early anti-lynching efforts, published in *The Journal of Negro History*, she said the organization's campaign had begun in 1911, and she credited its activities and investigations for revealing the falsity of the rape charge, and the fact that lynchings led to more general lawlessness. Ovington also documented how in the early years, 'much of the best work...was done by women.' Three were mentioned for special commendation: Ida was not one of them." Wells-Barnett's relationship with the newly-formed NAACP can be found in Chapter 6. Her "invisibility" in the lynching struggle can be found in Chapter 8, and her complicated relationships with white feminists can be found in Chapter 9.

47. Giddings, pp. 560-562.

48. Ida Wells-Barnett (1917). *The East St. Louis Massacre: The Greatest Outrage of the Century* (Chicago: The Negro Fellowship Herald Press). As quoted in Bay, pp. 493-494.

49. Giddings, pp. 566-574.

50. Ida Wells-Barnett (1920). *The Arkansas Race Riot,* self-published, as quoted in Bay, p. 553.

51. Duster, p. 81.

52. Rosalyn Terborg-Penn, *African American Women in the Struggle for the Vote, 1850-1920* (Bloomington and Indianapolis: Indiana University Press, 1998), p. 97. (The NACW, which Wells would later help found, is discussed in Chapter 6.) Terborg-Penn adds on page 100 that

in New York City, at least, there was some hope of inter-racial work, albeit somewhat Jim Crowed: "Black women suffragists mobilized in New York City boroughs in the 1890s, as indicated previously in the discussion of the Women's Loyal Union. However the Black woman suffrage network in New York City broadened as white suffragists in the city realized the importance of African American men who voted and the political awareness of their women. As early as 1910, white women suffragists from several organizations worked with African-American clubwomen, asking them to form 'colored' chapters of various suffrage associations."

53. Frederick Douglass letter to *The New York Age*. Letter dated October 25, 1892. As reprinted as Introduction to Ida B. Wells' *Southern Horrors: Lynch Law in All its Phases* (1892), as published in Bay, p. 59.

54. In 2017, the organization is called the NACWC, the National Association of

Colored Women's Clubs. Its website is: http://www.nacwc.org/ .

55. Giddings, p. 376. It is worth noting that at that founding meeting, Wells-Barnett fought to use the term "Afro-American" in the group's title, instead of "Colored." She lost. The rejected term would gain prominence among Black Americans in the 1960s and early 1970s.

56. Duster, pp. 345-346.

57. Giddings, p. 282.

58. Giddings, p. 474.

59. *Ibid.*

60. *Ibid.*

61. *Ibid.,* p. 475.

62. W.E.B. Du Bois, "National Committee on the Negro," as quoted by Giddings, 476. Du Bois's essay can be found in Herbert Aptheker's *A Documentary History* book series.

63. Duster, p. 325, as quoted in Giddings, p. 477.

64. As quoted in Giddings, p. 478.
65. *Ibid.*
66. *Ibid.*, p. 479.
67. *Ibid.*
68. As quoted in Giddings, p. 480.
69. *Ibid.*, p. 497.
70. *Ibid.*, p. 411. This alienation extended even to the Ida B. Wells Club, Chicago Black women's organization that bore Wells-Barnett's name, although Giddings (pp. 439-440) named Wells-Barnett's autocratic attitude as the culprit. "As Ida recounted in her autobiography, the rupture occurred when the IBW Club was invited by Mary V. Plummer, the white reformer who had been secretary of the Chicago Anti-Lynching League, to become a member of the predominately white League of Cook County Clubs, an organization dedicated to coordinating the work of women's organizations. The invitation also included a spot on the league's board, and Ida,

without informing [IBW President and NACW Vice President Agnes] Moody, hastily accepted the offer and the board position. The IBW president was understandably furious and apparently did not accept the explanation that there was a pressing deadline to accept the position and that she was unable to contact Moody (no one in the group had telephones at the time Ida noted.) There is no indication that the rift was healed before Moody, who had a history of heart problems, died in 1903, and it can be reasonably assumed that Wells-Barnett's behavior did little to endear her to other members of the IBW or the other clubs."

71. *Ibid.*

72. Duster, p. 306.

73. Duster, p. xxv.

74. Douglass did speak with his usual power and grace. In the audience was a young Black man named Robert Sengstacke Abbott, who was deeply moved and in-

spired. He would found *The Chicago Defender*—a crusading Black newspaper that Wells-Barnett would in her later years write for—in 1905.

75. See the National Urban League's annual *State of Black America* book-length report, and/or activist-broadcaster Tavis Smiley's *The Covenant with Black America* book-length reports for modern-day versions of this kind of document. Perhaps the most famous 20th century Black political report is the document produced by the National Black Political Convention in Gary, Indiana in 1972.

76. The Afterword of Decosta-Willis' *Diary* (p. 194) has an interview with Alfreda Duster, Wells-Barnett's daughter and biographer. She said of her parents: "She used to make bread, but my dad did most of the cooking. He liked to cook—she didn't—so he'd go into the kitchen, put on an apron. He always had to have at least two different types of meat on the table—sometimes three. One wasn't enough. Dad loved stews and

hash, didn't do too much frying. When I got big enough, I was supposed to help. I made corn pone every night—a mixture of corn meal and water. You make patties and cook them in hot grease. My father usually came home first, on the streetcar. I watched from the window so I could start the corn pone."

77. Duster, p. 255. The chapter of Wells' autobiography that carries this exchange is called "Divided Duty." Giddings, a modern Black feminist historian, relayed this story in a chapter notably called "Undivided Duty." Said Giddings (p. 390), who quoted Wells-Barnett's autobiography, of the encounter: "Wells-Barnett characterized Anthony's words as a 'well-merited rebuke,' adding that she could not tell the aging suffragist that 'I had been able, unlike herself, to get the support which was necessary to carry on my work [and] that I had become discouraged in the effort to carry on alone.' That exchange, Ida implied, made her decide to fully—and unapolo-

getically—reenter public life, if only to 'help unite our people so that there would be a following to help in the arduous work necessary.'" I think it also shows how little support Wells-Barnett received from white suffragists as well as from elements of the Black community.

78. As quoted by Giddings, p. 294.

79. *Ibid.*

80. *Ibid.*

81. *Ibid.*

82. Ibid., p. 304. Giddings wrote that Douglass told Aked that he had gotten a cable-gram asking if he endorsed Wells. He said, "I gave the answer that I endorsed *the mission* [my emphasis], I do this entirely."

83. *Ibid.*, pp. 294-295.

84. *Ibid.*, as quoted by and in Giddings, pp. 294-295.

85. *Ibid.*, p. 656.

86. *Ibid.*, p. 658.
87. Terborg-Penn, p. 2.
88. Giddings, p. 350.
89. *Ibid.*
90. *Ibid.*
91. *Ibid.*
92. Duster, p. 230.
93. *Ibid.*
94. Jane Addams, "Respect For Law," *The Independent*, January 3, 1901, as typed here: http://hullhouse.uic.edu/hull/urbanexp/main.cgi?file=viewer.ptt&mime=blank&doc=326&type=print.
95. Ida B. Wells-Barnett, "Lynching and the Excuse For It," *The Independent,* May 16, 1901, as published in Mia Bay, p. 409.
96. *Ibid.*, pp. 409-410.
97. Giddings, pp. 514-519.
98. Terborg-Penn, p. 123.

99. Giddings, p. 584.

100. Giddings, p. 590.

101. Trotter stowed away on a ship, and went anyway. As Giddings (p. 590) told the tale: "Upon his arrival, he began churning out petitions and news releases, which were picked up by the French press, that detailed the discriminatory treatment accorded Black soldiers and the brutality African Americans faced at home."

102. De Priest would later that year run for Congress, and become the first Black person to be elected to it in the 20th century. Ironically, Wells-Barnett was familiar with De Priest, since she helped start his career; in 1915, she and the Alpha Suffragist Club helped elect De Priest to an alderman slot.

103. Duster, pp. 418-419.

104. That book is Jacqueline Jones Royster's (ed.) (1996). *Southern Horrors and Other Writings: The Anti-Lynching Campaign*

of Ida B. Wells (New York: Bedford/ St. Martin's, 1996).

105. They are: Giddings, *Sword*; Mia Bay's *To Tell The Truth Freely: The Life of Ida B. Wells* (New York: Hill and Wang, 2010); Patricia A. Schechter's intellectual history, *Ida B. Wells-Barnett and American Reform, 1880-1930* (Chapel Hill, N.C.: University of North Carolina Press, 2001), and Linda McMurray's *To Keep The Waters Troubled: The Life of Ida B. Wells* (Oxford: Oxford University Press, 1999). The compilation of Wells' writings is Bay's (ed.) (2014) *The Light of Truth*.

BIBLIOGRAPHY

Books

Bay, Mia (ed.), *Ida B. Wells: The Light of Truth: Writings of an Anti-Lynching Crusader*. (New York: Penguin Books, 2014).

Bennett, Lerone Jr., *The Shaping of Black America*. (New York: Penguin Books, 1993 reprint of 1991 revised ed.).

DeCosta-Willis, Miriam (ed), *The Memphis Diary of Ida B. Wells: An Intimate Portrait of the Activist as a Young Woman*. (Boston: Beacon Press, 1995).

Duster, Alfreda M. (ed.), *Crusade for Justice: The Autobiography of Ida B. Wells*. (Chicago and London: University of Chicago Press, 1970).

Giddings, Paula, *A Sword Among Lions: Ida B. Wells and the Campaign Against Lynching*. (New York: Amistad, 2008).

———, *Where and When I Enter: The Impact of Black Women on Race and Sex in America*. (New York: William Morrow and Co., 1984).

McMurray, Linda O. *To Keep the Waters Troubled: The Life of Ida B. Wells*. (New York: Oxford University Press, 1998).

Rhodes, Jane, *Mary Ann Shadd Cary: The Black Press and Protest in the Nineteenth Century*. (Bloomington, Ind.: Indiana University Press, 1998).

Streitmatter, Rodger, *Raising Her Voice: African-American Women Journalists Who Changed History*. (Lexington: University of Kentucky, 1994).

Terborg-Penn, Rosalyn, *African American Women in the Struggle for the Vote, 1850-1920*. (Bloomington and Indianapolis: Indiana University Press, 1998).

Articles

Addams, Jane, "Respect For Law," *The Independent*, January 3, 1901.

http://hullhouse.uic.edu/hull/urbanexp/
main.cgi?file=viewer.ptt&mime=blank&
doc=326&type=print.

Unpublished Dissertations

Burroughs, Todd Steven, "Drums In The Global Village: Toward an Ideological History of Black Media," Unpublished dissertation. College Park: University of Maryland at College Park, 2001.

ABOUT THE AUTHOR

TODD STEVEN BURROUGHS, Ph.D., is an independent researcher and writer based in Newark, N.J. He has taught at Howard University, the nation's top historically Black university, in Washington, D.C., and Morgan State University, Maryland's top historically Black college, in Baltimore, Maryland. A professional journalist since 1985, he has written for *The Source, ColorLines, Black Issues Book Review* and *The Crisis* magazines, websites such as *BlackAmericaWeb.com* and *TheRoot.com* and newspapers such as *The New York Amsterdam News*, the New Jersey edition of *The Afro-American* newspaper chain and *The* (Newark, N.J.) *Star-Ledger*, New Jersey's largest newspaper. He served as an editor, contributing columnist and national correspondent for the NNPA News Service (*www.nnpa.org; www.BlackPressUSA.com*), the nation's only newswire for Black newspapers. Burroughs, a Ph.D. in Communication from the University of Maryland's Philip Merrill College of Journalism, is a lifelong student of the history of Black media. He is the author of an audiobook, *Son-Shine On Cracked Side-*

walks, which deals with the 2014 mayoral election of Ras Baraka, the son of the late activist and writer Amiri Baraka, in Newark, N.J. The co-author with Herb Boyd of *Civil Rights: Yesterday and Today* and co-editor, with Jared A. Ball, of *A Lie of Reinvention: Correcting Manning Marable's Malcolm X*, he is currently co-writing a book, with Wayne J. Dawkins, on *Freedomways* magazine. This is his first solo-authored book.

CPSIA information can be obtained
at www.ICGtesting.com
Printed in the USA
FSHW020810180919
62123FS